Karen,

It's a pleasure
working with you.
Best wishes in improving
the patient sat. scores!

Theo

The Six Principles of Service Excellence

A Proven Strategy for Driving
World-Class Employee Performance
and Elevating the Customer Experience
from Average to Extraordinary

By

Theo Gilbert-Jamison

authorHOUSE™

1663 LIBERTY DRIVE, SUITE 200
BLOOMINGTON, INDIANA 47403
(800) 839-8640
WWW.AUTHORHOUSE.COM

First published by AuthorHouse 07/29/05

ISBN: 1-4208-5630-8 (sc)
ISBN: 1-4208-5631-6 (dj)

Library of Congress Control Number: 2005904450

Printed in the United States of America
Bloomington, Indiana

This book is printed on acid-free paper.

ACKNOWLEDGEMENTS

Having worked on this book during the past eighteen months, it would not be possible without the support of my closest friends, colleagues, and family members to get my concepts and thoughts from my mind to paper so that they may be applied universally.

Many people in my life were part of this journey with me. I would like to especially thank the following individuals:

Charles Josey – for his skill and expertise
in helping me write this book

Vivian Bright - for her leadership skill and wisdom

Linda Conway – for her creativity and insight

Mike Jamison – for his support and encouragement

Andrea Gilbert and Sandra Simpson
– for their consistent prayers

Kathy Allen – for being an extremely supportive great friend

The Heavenly Creator – for inspiring
me to write this body of work

TABLE OF CONTENTS

INTRODUCTION

> *Becoming the undisputed leader in customer service, performance excellence, and quality does not occur by chance. It takes the full commitment of senior leadership, a sound strategy, and adequate internal resources* (the right people, work processes, tools, and technology), *all aligned system-wide to create a superior level of service that is sustainable.*

Business Context

Every company in every industry is, of course, seeking ways to improve bottom-line results. Most, however, are passing up the opportunity of benefiting from creating loyal customers through service excellence. While they see that stellar customer service is delivering enviable rewards for others, they either believe it is not applicable to their situation or that they are unable to duplicate the achievement within their own organizations. Thankfully, an increasing number of business leaders want to know how to replicate service excellence in their organizations. I know this is true because, in my seventeen-year career with The Ritz-Carlton Hotel Company, the first question inevitably asked me following a keynote speech was "How do you do it?"

This book answers that question by providing a step-by-step process that assures success when followed to the letter. Not only is it successful in the hospitality industry, it is equally successful in every business field and in every size profit-oriented and non-profit operation.

I am delighted that so many want to know the process and that leaders are awakening to the fact that excellent customer service is part of a chain reaction that creates a series of desirable conditions: smoother operation, employee loyalty, and customer loyalty. The loyalty of both your people and your customer base are two key ingredients of financial stability and profitability. Unfortunately, few companies are willing to invest the necessary time and funding crucial to making changes that generate these lasting, desirable, profitable results. In other words, service excellence does have its start-up costs; however, once in place it pays great dividends.

Improving service in any organization involves more than merely sending employees to a one-to-two hour traditional customer service class to learn how to smile and be nice. And, sadly, that is all most customer service classes are capable of delivering. Unquestionably, improving front line service involves a more comprehensive approach to resolving systemic work environment issues and cannot be successful without 100 percent endorsement and commitment – not just lip service – from senior leadership.

Imagine arriving at work and not having to worry about day-to-day pressures and frustrating issues such as:

- Will my employees show up today, 100 percent committed to providing quality work?

- Will they have the necessary resources and tools to deliver excellence?

- Do we have enough staff to get the job done?

- Why don't my employees clearly understand their role in consistently delivering exceptional service?

- What will my customers be upset about today?

- Will my boss recognize the hard work of our team or come down hard on us again for not making budget this month?

Imagine a work environment where leaders are able to truly focus on delivering excellence through continuous improvement of their products and services, while their employees are empowered to delight customers, as well as effectively and without incident resolve customer problems, issues or challenges that arise. All that can be yours. Again and again, I have seen that, when leaders become fully engaged, they are capable of creating a work environment in which a culture of Service Excellence Workshop thrives. As the model below suggests, leadership engagement has a direct impact on service excellence and, consequently, on profitability.

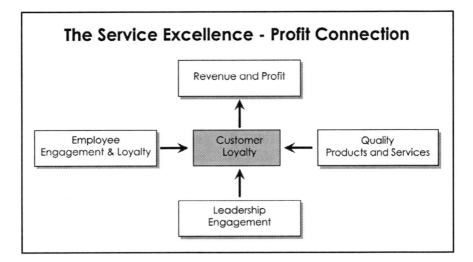

Purpose

The purpose of this book is to surface the root causes of mediocre employee performance *(which translates to poor customer service)* and to clarify the principles that drive world-class performance and foster a culture of service excellence. As you explore the process, you will discover how six common principles can help leaders create a fully engaged, self-motivated, and empowered workforce.

While many companies seek the easy alternatives or shortcuts to improving customer service, there is *one best way* for companies that are serious about becoming unrivaled leaders in their industries. This "one best way" incorporates a systematic, comprehensive series of steps that, if followed without hesitation, will over time elevate any organization to world-class status, recognition, customer and employee loyalty, and increased revenue and profitability.

Perhaps this is the point to say that service excellence is not and should not be identical in all organizations. The level of service you expect to experience at a medical facility is quite different from what would be most desirable at a bank or a grocery store. For each there is an ultimate experience. However, the same process applies to creating an ultimate experience, no matter what product or service is being delivered. No matter the field, *The Six Principles of Service Excellence* presents a simple yet comprehensive approach to improving employee performance in order to achieve bottom-line results. While these six principles are not foreign or new to most companies, there are very few who practice consistent application. Therefore, there are few who go on to achieve world-renowned recognition for product and service excellence, the precursors of market domination.

Each of the Six Principles is a significant milestone; therefore, a typical reaction of organizations going through this process is to get so excited after completing the initial step that they do not complete the process. However, world-class service and customer loyalty can only be achieved and consistently delivered by completing the entire process.

The Best Way to Benefit from this Book

This book shares much information based on practical, common sense lessons I learned during my years with The Ritz-Carlton Hotel Company and while consulting with other fine organizations. You can also benefit from this learning by making three commitments: (1) to being open to changing your paradigms about leadership, employee accountability, service, and excellence; (2) to sharing the knowledge you gain from this book with others on your team; and (3) to substituting talk with action and maximizing your efforts by immediately implementing what you learn.

To heighten your learning experience, this book is divided into four distinct sections.

- **Part 1** of *The Six Principles of Service Excellence* covers vision, mission, business objectives, and service standards. It takes us through the methodology of creating the basis for a culture of service excellence by strengthening all employees' understanding of your organization's service philosophy, goals and of the path that leads to achieving them.

- **Part 2** focuses on intervention, learning strategy and organizational alignment. Here, we look at all of the necessary components and implementation strategy for sustaining a culture of service excellence.

- **Part 3** involves measurement and leadership accountability. In this section, we focus on creating a measurement system to hold leadership accountable for service excellence. This is necessary to create credibility and determine the return on investment of your service excellence initiative.

- **Part 4** provides leaders with the necessary mindset to drive service excellence. Here we examine the role of the leader in achieving service excellence, as well as how you can apply *The Six Principles of Service Excellence* in your personal life.

My hope is that this book, *The Six Principles of Service Excellence,* becomes your benchmark for improving the products, services, and financial viability of your organization. It is a proven recipe, and like all recipes, the desired outcome requires that all ingredients be added to the mix in a precise order. When they are, the result is virtually a magic potion with lasting results.

— ◈ —

THE SIX PRINCIPLES OVERVIEW
Chapter 1

> *The bottom line is that achieving service excellence is not something you do once or once in a while; it must be constantly tended, if you want it to continue and help you achieve higher profits and dominance in your field.*

I always open my presentations and speeches by asking two questions: (1) What are some of the customer service challenges you face, as a leader? and (2) What processes have you implemented to overcome these challenges and hold employees accountable for consistently delivering exceptional service?

After giving me blank stares, most of the attendees' responses are around *making* employees do specific things, such as smile, be nice to the customer, and go above and beyond. Unfortunately, unless you watch an employee every minute and carry a loaded gun, you cannot *make* employees do anything. Furthermore, an insincere smile or greeting is just as bad as none at all. Employees have to *want* to deliver exceptional service and have to be held accountable for delivering it.

Just about every leader is searching for a more effective way to manage his or her department, minimize expenses and costs, and provide better service to customers. However, with so many organizational issues to juggle at any given time *(staffing, cost, productivity, quality, and more),* it becomes increasingly difficult to expend much effort solely on elevating customer service – especially to the level of excellence.

I have heard it argued – and so have you – that service excellence is something that is not really expected from companies or firms other than the posh, high-end operations that cater to the elite, that small percentage of the market willing to pay a substantial price for what they receive. In other words, it is just fancy fluff for the few; that's often the assertion. But is that true?

I asked a colleague to list some companies, stores, and other businesses that he feels deliver exceptional service. I found some of the examples he immediately offered surprising and others not so surprising. One of his examples was a sizeable bank where the tellers and branch managers make an effort to know their customers by name. "That may not seem like a big issue," my friend said, "but I like the fact that they know me on sight, smile, and seem eager to be helpful." He added, "It, also, doesn't hurt that the bank keeps a carafe of fresh, hot coffee and a tray of freshly baked, continually restocked cookies in the lobby. Clearly, these people want my business, and, thanks to them, I actually enjoy going to the bank."

The Roadmap to Service Excellence

While every organization's roadmap to achieving service excellence includes some common elements, the journey is unique to each organization. For some, there are areas where they are already extremely strong. I call these *pockets of excellence.* However, every organization also has weak spots, often referred to as *gaps* or *barriers.* The key is to identify the gaps that are preventing you from consistently achieving service excellence and to implement effective interventions to eliminate and close those gaps forever. In turn, you create not just pockets of excellence, but a culture deeply immersed in building customer loyalty.

Following a recent seminar, a lady shared with me an analogy that has merit; so, pardon me if I mix metaphors and offer it as well. She asked, "Have you ever seen a plate spinner at a circus or carnival? He balances a china plate on a flexible pole, gives it a spin and then moves on to the next pole and the next, setting a plate on each and setting it in motion."

I, immediately, saw where she was headed. The plate spinner has little trouble getting the first two or three plates spinning; however, as he moves on down the line, adding plate after plate, the first ones begin to wobble a bit. Unless he dashes back and gives each periodic spins, they lose momentum and crash to the floor.

Therefore, the plate spinner has to tend to his entire set of spinning plates, continually making certain that not a single one loses its momentum and topples.

Think of the eight points I am about to list as spinning plates that must be kept in motion or as milestones that must be reached daily. The bottom line is that achieving service excellence is not something you do once or once in a while; it is something you must constantly tend if you want it to achieve higher profits and dominance in your field.

So, what are the eight milestones that must be passed regularly? You must have:

1. high **Customer Loyalty;**

2. a strong **Service Culture and Philosophical Values;**

3. an effective **Leadership Development Program;**

4. an effective process to enhance the **Skills and Knowledge** of your employees;

5. a strong **Selection Process** that is linked to the philosophical values of your organization;

6. **Departmental Accountability** for maintaining a strong service culture;

7. high **Quality** of products and services through **Continuous Improvement;**

8. a **Work Environment** that fosters synergy and encourages **Teamwork.**

Service Excellence Defined

I often describe service excellence as being a *journey*, not a *destination* because the pursuit of service excellence never ends. It is also not something that you do to people; it is a goal that you attain with people. Service excellence is often interpreted in different ways. For the purposes of alignment, we define it as:

- *An intrinsic desire to go above and beyond to please and delight the customer;*

- *Consistently enhancing the service experience for the customer;*

- *Investing in the proper resources, systems, and processes to support this concept (selection, skill/knowledge, work environment, reward and recognition);*

- *Creating a culture of continuous improvement; it cannot be perceived as a program of the month;*

- *Commitment, support, and involvement from the top; if the CEO and senior leadership do not embrace this concept, it will be difficult to drive service excellence throughout the organization;*

- *Using your customer and employee satisfaction survey feedback to elevate service levels;*

- *Fostering a work environment that creates high employee loyalty;*

- *Focusing on customer loyalty versus customer satisfaction.*

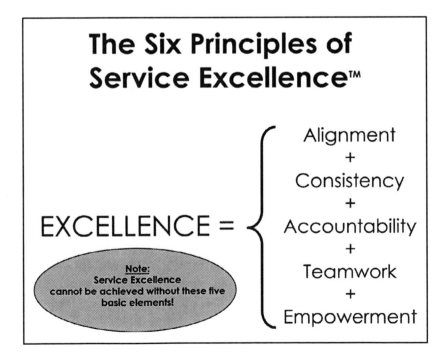

The Six Principles of Service Excellence™

EXCELLENCE =

Note:
Service Excellence cannot be achieved without these five basic elements!

Alignment
+
Consistency
+
Accountability
+
Teamwork
+
Empowerment

Simply defined, service excellence is the sum total of alignment, consistency, accountability, teamwork, and empowerment. This means that, in order to achieve service excellence, an organization's employees must be united. They must have a clear understanding of, agree with, and value the service philosophy and business priorities set by the organization. Next, there must be consistent processes in place system-wide for supporting service excellence. There is no room at any level for compromise or excuses. There must also be a spirit of collaboration and teamwork so that employees are inspired to take initiative or *action* to do the things that are necessary to elevate the customer's service experience.

Grounded in Experience

The Six Principles model is based on more than my experience as Vice President of Training and Organizational Effectiveness for The Ritz-Carlton Hotel Company. Also, supporting the model is work I have done with other organizations since launching my consulting firm, as well as my analysis of how companies that I have carefully studied deliver exceptional service. So, we will not be taking a journey to some business fantasyland. Instead, we will focus on real-life scenarios in businesses that deliver products and services that are similar to yours.

The Six Principles Model

As I analyzed one organization after another at the top of its industry in service, customer loyalty, and eventually profitability, I discovered the same six principles at work. In fact, despite continual searching for exceptions to this model, I found none. The model was the same in every successful case. And in every successful case, these principles have led to a sustainable financial success. While I will not be dwelling on the issue of profit, let me assure you that if these principles did not contribute substantially to a user's bottom line, I would not waste time trying to convince you they have merit. Financial success is more than highly desirable; it is absolutely essential. I cannot imagine a company being in business just to be liked.

In this chapter, we have a brief overview of The Six Principles model. The following chapters present an in-depth view of each individual principle, how each principle works, and why each is important. In other words, this chapter identifies the potential pitfalls, while the remaining chapters explore means of avoiding the pitfalls.

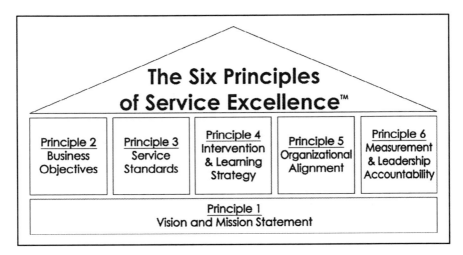

Principle 1 - Vision and Mission

The foundation of *The Six Principles of Service Excellence* is the philosophical values of an organization: vision and mission. Every operation wanting to drive service and performance excellence must have a vision and mission with which employees can emotionally connect and embrace. While an organization can survive years without ever attempting to define or clarify what its unique purpose is, those interested in elevating the customer experience to a level that surpasses their competition must eventually face this juncture.

> A *vision statement* should clearly communicate the *desired* or *future* state of your organization

A strong written vision statement is not enough; your employees must also view the stated vision as *attainable*. You can say that your vision is to be the most trusted bank in the world or the manufacturer of the most reliable automobile ever made or to be the most revered law firm on the planet; however, if your employees consider the chances of that vision becoming reality less likely than their chances of winning the lottery five weeks in a row, your vision will not be achieved.

How Vision and Mission Statements Differ
A *vision statement* defines what you *want* to become
A *mission statement* articulates the *purpose* of the organization

---

While vision and mission statements work in tandem, they serve different purposes. Think of your mission statement as a gauge or compass by which your most important business decisions should be evaluated and determined. In other words, your vision states where you aspire to go, while your mission statement tells how you plan to get there. Chapter Three is dedicated to providing in-depth information to help you assess the relevance and effectiveness of your organization's current vision and mission statements and potentially create new statements that will drive world-class employee performance and service excellence.

Principle 2 - Business Objectives

Many organizations do not include service excellence goals in their business objectives and strategic plans. Subsequently, service excellence does not become a high priority for departments, work teams or individual employees. This occurs when service quality becomes secondary or disassociated with revenue and profit goals, as if service excellence has no appreciable affect on the financial success of a business.

If an organization is striving to elevate the service experience of its customers, then ambitious service excellence objectives might be to: Increase Customer Loyalty by 10%; Increase Employee Loyalty by 25%; Reduce Employee Turnover by 15%; Reduce Customer Problems or Complaints; or Increase Quality of Services or Product.

In order to have any meaning, these goals or objectives must be quantifiable. It is also important for the workforce to be aligned with the business objectives that relate to achieving service excellence and with their individual and team roles in reaching the objectives. *Aligned* in this sense means employees clearly understand what the goals are and know specifically what *they* need to do individually or as a team, in order to contribute to the success of the organization. Elevating employee consciousness to this higher level of thinking is a challenge we will tackle in Chapter Four. For now, remember that achieving alignment is not optional; it is a critical requirement.

Principle 3 - Service Standards

Service standards should not be confused with brand standards. Many organizations have brand standards; few also have service standards.

- **Service standards** specify the behavior employees are expected to exemplify to ensure the customer consistently receives flawless service. *Example: Every customer who enters our facility is immediately acknowledged and warmly greeted with a smile at the instant of contact.*

- **Brand standards** typically specify types of equipment or processes that must be used system-wide. *Example: The standard company flag (4' x 6') must be displayed at the entrance of every facility. Frayed or soiled flags are replaced at once.*

One of the primary reasons many organizations struggle with aligning their workforce with their philosophical values is they have no consistent service standards that define what behaviors are expected of everyone. In this book, you will encounter the following words more than once: *Never assume employees know what to do.* Only through open, effective communication, training and empowerment will they learn. Only after becoming engaged through "buy-in" will employees consistently deliver exceptional service.

Chapter Five provides you with the insight necessary to quickly assess the relevance and effectiveness of your organization's current service standards. There, you will also create new service standards to help your employees more closely mirror the organizational vision and mission statements in their everyday interactions with the customer.

Principle 4 – Intervention and Learning Strategy

Once the vision and mission, business objectives, and service standards have been solidified, there must be a strategy outlining how they will be woven into every aspect of the organization's culture. Employee training and development as an intervention is often the low hanging fruit, the easy win; so, it is an appropriate initial intervention. However, a thorough gap analysis inevitably reveals other areas where the service excellence interventions can have a significant affect.

The purpose of the service excellence gap analysis is to identify barriers, beyond training, that impede your workforce's ability to deliver an unparalleled service experience to the customer every day. I often ask leaders to consider and list those things that are currently preventing them, their department, or their employees from providing consistent superior service. As you go through this book, I highly recommend you do the same and jot down a list of gaps you face. We will uncover the best approaches for closing service gaps in Chapter Six.

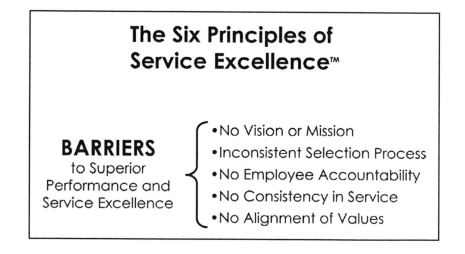

The Six Principles of Service Excellence™

BARRIERS
to Superior
Performance and
Service Excellence

- No Vision or Mission
- Inconsistent Selection Process
- No Employee Accountability
- No Consistency in Service
- No Alignment of Values

Principle 5 - Organizational Alignment

To create sustainability, it is extremely important that we find effective ways to positively rally the workforce around the philosophical values *(vision and mission)* and objectives of the organization. A lasting bond must be developed. Without organizational alignment, none of these desirable outcomes stands a chance of being fully realized.

Some organizations use daily pre-shift meetings, often referred to as *daily line-ups*. While this is a great concept and may work very effectively in organizations such as The Ritz-Carlton, daily line-ups are not quite suited for others. There are numerous other innovative and traditional methods of aligning your organizations outlined in Chapter Seven.

Certainly, there is no reason to reinvent the wheel – especially if your company already has effective communication mechanisms in place that can be used to consistently align the workforce with service excellence. However, occasionally augmenting your traditional forms of communication with something fresh and unexpected can make a strong impression on your people. Chapter Seven also uncovers how to assess the effectiveness of your current internal communication scheme and determine new ways to align your workforce with service excellence.

Principle 6 - Measurement and Leadership Accountability

To create credibility around your service excellence initiative, senior leadership must be able to determine the return on investment or the value of the initiative on which they have embarked. During this final process, a Service Excellence Scorecard is developed to help measure your ability to achieve the business objectives. This scorecard is critical to holding leadership accountable for driving and supporting your organization's entire service excellence initiative.

The ultimate goal of measurement is to ensure consistency, leadership accountability and team recognition. It often takes a few months to develop and refine a scorecard that will be effective within your organization. But over time, it can become a very powerful tool for quantifying and visually communicating the success or failure of the initiative. Chapter Eight will help you assess the effectiveness of your current organizational scorecard and ensure there are relevant metrics that focus on continuous improvement and leadership accountability.

Service Excellence Study

In a study of the organizations my firm, Performance Solutions by Design, worked with during a twelve month period, the data revealed was astounding. I will refer to this data repeatedly throughout the remainder of this book as I walk you through *The Six Principles of Service Excellence* and continue reinforcing the significance of leadership and employee engagement in creating the ultimate service experience for the customer.

- *Vision Statements* – 91 percent of the organizations polled had no vision statement. Therefore, their employees had no idea of where the organization is going in the future or what it aspires to be.

- *Mission Statements* – 88 percent of organizations polled had a mission statement. However, after conducting an in-depth gap analysis, 66 percent found that their mission statement was no longer relevant in relation to their elevated service expectations.

- *Business Objectives* – 100 percent of organizations polled had business objectives. However, only in 22 percent of these organizations are the objectives shared with the most valuable people, their employees.

- *Service Standards* - Only 22 percent of the organizations polled had relevant service standards. Unfortunately, most organizations confuse service standards with brand standards. As noted earlier, service standards address the "key touch points" of the service experience that ultimately delight the customer, while brand standards deal with ensuring that the physical aspects *(furnishings, equipment, software)* of the business are consistent.

- *Intervention and Learning Strategy* - Only 11 percent of the organizations polled integrated their service philosophy as part of their foundational human resource practices (New Hire Interview Process, New Employee Orientation, Technical and Soft Skills Training, Leadership Development, Performance Review Process, Reward and Recognition Programs). Also, in only 5 percent of organizations polled were service excellence initiatives recognized as part of their annual company-wide strategic plan.

- *Organizational Alignment* - Only 5 percent of organizations polled had a consistent, effective process for continuously aligning employees with the function and purpose of their jobs, which is to deliver unparalleled service every day.

- *Measurement and Leadership Accountability* – 89 percent of organizations polled did not use Customer Satisfaction Survey and Employee Satisfaction Survey data to measure their ability to delight and exceed customer expectations. Because they collected no customer or employee satisfaction data, they had no basis for determining how well they were or were not doing.

Life Application of The Six Principles

The simplest way to apply The Six Principles is to look at them from a personal perspective. Everyone I know shares a common vision of being healthy and physically fit. To achieve this vision, we typically set out with a mission to exercise more and lose weight. If we seek the assistance of a nutritional expert or fitness trainer, he or she helps set realistic goals to succeed in our vision and mission. After that, it is truly up to us to implement the necessary interventions in the form of an action plan for reaching our vision of being healthy and physically fit. These interventions may be to walk or jog and eat right, but if we do not commit to these activities regularly, our results will be minimal at best.

To stay focused, we may align ourselves with others who are also in pursuit of the same health and fitness vision. Most of all, we use the measurement goal of losing 10, 15 or 20 pounds as an indicator of our success and routinely weigh ourselves to track our progress. If you look at The Six Principles from this perspective, it is very similar to life principles that we use each day.

Just as there is no short cut or quick fix when it comes to sustaining a healthy, fit lifestyle, there is also no quick fix when it comes to sustaining service excellence. While there are a vast number of diet pills on the market that you can pop daily to lose weight, if you do not incorporate regular exercise in your regimen, the weight will slowly return. Also, most diet pills do not claim to make you healthier. Likewise, to achieve a culture of service excellence, leadership must be committed to creating a healthy work environment where it can thrive; this takes a comprehensive approach and leads to sustainability.

Key Points

- Service excellence does not happen by chance. However, you can achieve it through the comprehensive, systematic approach of *The Six Principles of Service Excellence.*

- Service excellence starts with highly engaged employees who have an intrinsic desire to go above and beyond to take care of and delight the customer.

- Service excellence is not a give-away; it is a customer and profit magnet. It draws loyal customers to your organization or establishment, generates pride in employees, and builds your company a lasting reputation and level of respect that no amount of public relations and advertising dollars can create on their own.

- Service excellence is that genuine quality that all customers want to discover in the companies and organizations with which they do business. Once you create an on-going culture of service excellence, your marketing agencies' job becomes a breeze.

- Your customers may not be able to define service excellence off the top of their heads or even in 25 or less carefully selected words; however, they know it when they see it, and they love it when they personally experience it. Service excellence is addictive; so, they return again and again. Yes, addictive. The addictiveness of service excellence is what customer loyalty is all about.

—◈—

THE FOUNDATION FOR
A CULTURE OF SERVICE
EXCELLENCE
Chapter 2

Customer service is about maintaining the status quo in service. Service excellence is about taking the customer experience to an unparalleled level.

The Leadership Mindset Necessary
to Embrace this Body of Work

This book is written specifically for leaders who are consumed with excellence. This includes senior executives, division heads, middle managers, and supervisors because every leadership level is accountable for service. My goal is to empower you with the skills and knowledge necessary to drive service excellence within your organization, division or even small work team. Over the years, I have found that leaders who easily embrace *The Six Principles of Service Excellence* concept possess nine fundamental characteristics.

1. **They are avid students of service excellence**, always striving for perfection in the manner in which service is delivered to the customer. They are never satisfied with mediocre or even good service, and persevere until they are able to consistently deliver the *ultimate customer experience*.

2. **They find meaning and purpose in their work,** and because of their strong drive towards the vision and mission, they easily inspire others to enthusiastically follow them.

3. **They receive an intrinsic satisfaction** from watching employees grow and thrive in a work environment that fosters empowerment and uncompromising levels of service for both internal and external customers.

4. **They stay focused on the big picture,** which is ultimately customer loyalty. The energy of their teams is channeled toward successful achievement of the business objectives.

5. **They have high expectations and set high standards** for their employees. Unwilling to compromise established service standards; they take ownership of their work *(good or bad)* and desire to work alongside other dedicated employees.

6. **They are highly competitive** and do not enjoy losing or coming in second place. Being number two is not an option in the minds of leaders consumed with excellence. Excellence is achieved through their desire to be number one.

7. **They know that their attitude *(good or bad)* sets the tone for the team.** These leaders are addicted to positive thinking and have no problem confronting negativity head on. Their positive, upbeat demeanor enables them to create great relationships with employees and customers alike.

8. **They are empathetic in their helpful approach with people.** Because of their genuine concern for others, they become fully engaged in the moment by listening with their ears and heart to find the essence of any customer or employee dissatisfaction. They are supportive of the uniqueness of others and emotionally sensitive.

9. **They have an intense desire to share knowledge** with their team. Each regularly collects information that may be beneficial toward increasing the performance of their team, and each enjoys opportunities to learn more about the business.

If this is the profile or mindset of most of the leaders within your organization, they will have no problem understanding *The Six Principles of Service Excellence* concept or supporting you in an endeavor to heighten customer service. This book is not, however, for cynics and skeptics who do not believe that service excellence can be achieved in their organizations. At best, the cynics and skeptics will search for holes in this concept and spend their time consumed with thinking up reasons why service excellence is not achievable. So, if your team of leaders consists mostly of cynics and skeptics, you face a long and rugged road to achieving service excellence. Indeed, it may not be possible. In Chapter Nine, we elaborate further on the role of the leader in achieving service excellence.

Rental Car Woes

Most of my professional career I have done a lot of traveling. Typically I am in a different city every week and often rent a car. It is amazing how we, *as consumers,* often gravitate to the big name chains, assuming service will be better. This is a common myth that is often perpetuated by misleading television, newspaper and magazine ads. The following story demonstrates what happens when service organizations neglect to hire leaders and employees who fit the profile that best supports a culture of service excellence.

While in Washington, DC on a six-day business trip, I rented a car from a well recognized establishment. Picking up the car was flawless. The rental office's sales representative was warm, friendly and accommodating, and the car was exactly what I expected. The initial service experience was exceptional, and I drove away very impressed. However, when I returned the car and was presented the bill by the express lane attendant, my excellent impression was shattered by a final charge of almost $800, double the amount I had anticipated. So, I went directly to the rental car office to find out why my bill was so high.

During a 15-minute wait for service, I reviewed the bill in detail and determined many of the charges were for amenities that I had assumed were basic services; however, there was a $17 charge for an additional driver, which I had neither requested nor initialed.

The customer service rep did allow me to explain my case, but afterward informed me that he could not rebate anything and showed me where I had signed my initials. When I pointed out that the additional driver charge was not initialed, he cited company policy and advised me that he could not rebate the $17 charge. Since he was not empowered to satisfy the customer, I did not argue with him; instead, I requested to see the manager.

Five minutes later the manager, who clearly did not appreciate being summoned from her busy work over a mere $17, appeared. Before I could state my case, her decision was made, and she repeated company policy concerning rebates. I told her it was unacceptable being charged for an additional driver when I had not requested the option; therefore, I was not going to pay the charge. She, then, came up with the excuse that once a charge is in the computer, they could not override the system and take it off. I calmly told her that was nonsense and that I was not going to pay. By then there were at least 15 impatient customers in line behind me; so, she had to do something. Without explanation, she disappeared into her office and returned five minutes later with a bill miraculously minus the $17 charge.

When I related this incident to my colleagues, the rental car company lost tens of thousands of dollars in future business from people who did not want to risk a similar experience.

First, let's look at the cold mathematics involved. Over an erroneous $17 charge, the rental agency lost my annual rental car business, which amounts to more than $8,000 a year. Since my business associates, who were told about the experience, are shying away from that particular rental car company, I would conservatively estimate another $80,000 a year was also lost. That one-year loss of $80,000 of business over a ten-year period mounts to almost one million dollars in revenue.

Second, in my opinion, all of the bantering was unnecessary; it wasted valuable time for both of us and irritated waiting customers. However, what if the sales rep had politely offered me alternatives at the beginning of our transaction? What if he told me what he *could* do instead of citing policy? What if the manager emerged from her office to apologize and rebate the $17 without question? Customers typically want fast, reliable service and expect alternatives, when a problem arises. They do not want to be constantly reminded of policies or limitations. Service excellence involves being creative and having the authority to positively resolve customer problems.

Incidents of this type, however, happen thousands of times daily, which is why companies are forced to spend millions of dollars to buy customer loyalty through frequent flyer programs and the like. The sad thing is that once a customer's impression is marred, it is nearly impossible to get him or her to enthusiastically return. Apparently, not only was the rental car employee disengaged, but he was also a mirror image of his manager.

Customer Service versus Service Excellence

To grasp the concept of *The Six Principles of Service Excellence*, it is first important to understand the difference between customer service and service excellence. Many organizations kick off customer service initiatives each year, only to fail miserably at enhancing the service experience for the customer. When I think about customer service versus service excellence, the following words come to mind:

Customer Service	Service Excellence
• Meeting customer expectations • Compliance with customer needs • Having a warm and friendly demeanor • Sticking strictly to company policy • Competent, knowledgeable employees • Intense focus on the technical function of the job	• Exceeding customer expectations • Compliance and anticipation of customer needs • Exceeding the standards to delight the customer • Being accommodating and flexible • Employees who are subject matter experts • Intense focus on the function and purpose of the job
At best, a focus on customer service will create customer satisfaction	An intense focus on service excellence will create a high level of customer loyalty

Customer service is about maintaining the status quo in service; being the same as your competition typically creates customer satisfaction. Service excellence is about taking the customer experience to an unparalleled level; exceeding what is typically offered by your competition creates customer loyalty.

I often use the school report card as an example to further explain the difference between service excellence and customer service. Most parents aspire for their children to bring home an "A" on their school report card; I equate this to achieving service excellence. So, when organizations aspire to achieve service excellence, they are going for the "A." On the other hand, when a child brings home a "B," it is still considered good; nonetheless, deep inside, the parent knows that their child is capable of doing better. I equate this to the organization that focuses on customer service. In other words, the "B" grade will only bring you satisfied customers. If this is enough, you will always be a good organization. However, you will never achieve greatness or world-wide recognition and dominance in service by merely satisfying the customer.

Your customers intuitively know the difference between good customer service and service excellence. They may not be able to articulate the difference, but they feel it from the time they walk into your establishment and sense its presence in every employee interaction, until the time they walk out your door. Therefore, it is extremely important that you create a work environment that focuses on service excellence and strives to consistently deliver the ultimate customer experience.

Customer Satisfaction versus Customer Loyalty

I learned through experience with The Ritz-Carlton Hotel Company that high customer loyalty is a by-product of achieving and sustaining service excellence. What many independent studies reveal, I saw first hand: a loyal customer is far more valuable than a satisfied customer because a loyal customer is ten times more likely to return to do business with you, ten times more likely to spend more money with you, and ten times more likely to recommend you, your products and services to others. *Consistently* exceeding the expectations of the customer, personalizing his or her service experience, and continuously improving your product or service so that it creates greater value for the customer produces a level of customer loyalty that cannot be matched by your competitor.

On the other hand, focusing merely on customer satisfaction will not create a loyal customer following. It will create a customer base that *likes* your products or services, but can easily be swayed by your competitor because the only clear differentiator may be location or pricing. To create customer satisfaction, three basic elements of the service experience are necessary, and, quite frankly, they are the minimum expectation from your customer. Satisfied customers expect a defect-free product, delivered by warm and friendly employees, and an easy and effective way to resolve problems, should they arise.

If it is that simple, why do so many organizations fail at consistently achieving customer loyalty? Think for a moment of an establishment *(a restaurant, dry cleaners or grocery store)* to which you are extremely loyal. Why are you so loyal to them? I am personally loyal to my favorite restaurant, grocery store, and dry cleaners not only because their products are of a high caliber but also because their employees go out of their way to recognize me as a repeat customer. They know my name, always remember something special about me *(such as my favorite beverage, my birthday, how I like my clothes laundered, or even my favorite vacation spot),* and they use this knowledge to make every interaction I have with them memorable. At these establishments, employee purpose extends beyond making me satisfied – that is any customer's expectation. They also want me to be loyal. Any mediocre organization can build customer satisfaction, but only exceptional organizations are able to heighten service to a level of excellence that gains and sustains customer loyalty.

Focus on Purpose Rather than Function

Service excellence cannot be achieved without people; those who understand the purpose and importance of providing exceptional service. The wise know that service excellence extends beyond only delighting the customer in front of the boss; they understand that it must be accomplished time and time again *(even in the absence of management)* if it is to create customer loyalty.

23

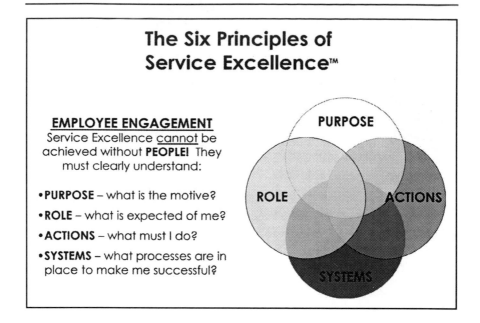

The Six Principles of Service Excellence™

EMPLOYEE ENGAGEMENT
Service Excellence <u>cannot</u> be achieved without **PEOPLE!** They must clearly understand:

- **PURPOSE** – what is the motive?
- **ROLE** – what is expected of me?
- **ACTIONS** – what must I do?
- **SYSTEMS** – what processes are in place to make me successful?

PURPOSE

ROLE

ACTIONS

SYSTEMS

An organization's ability to achieve and sustain service excellence is linked to leadership effectiveness and leaders' ability to fully engage their employees. The leader's role is to ensure employees understand their purpose, role, expected behaviors, and have the proper systems or processes in place to do quality work. To fully engage employees at this level, leaders must help them equally balance job function and purpose. When employees *only* focus on the functions of their job (the technical aspects), they often create a customer-*unfriendly* environment. Such employees are quick to quote company policy when there is a problem or situation involving customer dissatisfaction. They have the mindset that, *if it weren't for the customer, I could get my job done*, never fully realizing that if it weren't for the customer, they would never receive a paycheck.

Employees who focus on both the function and *purpose* of their work find meaning in their jobs. Their mindset extends beyond *just* being a waiter, housekeeper or cashier. They see themselves as service professionals and, therefore, willingly go above and beyond to take care of the customer. These employees are more apt to create a customer-*friendly* environment because they can easily put themselves in the shoes of the customer when they encounter a problem or instance of customer dissatisfaction. They have the mindset of high customer value, understanding that, *if it weren't for the customer, they would not have a job.*

The Six Principles of Service Excellence™

Leadership Function	Leadership Purpose
Manage and oversee department or division operations	Inspire, lead and motivate employees to achieve greater goals
Operate within budget	Set the vision and mission for the department, division or work team
Hire and manage employees	
Attend meetings	Be a mentor, coach and role model
Control costs and waste	Ensure the team is aligned around a common purpose
Maintain and improve worker productivity	Provide direction, praise and recognition for a job well done
Handle internal/external conflict	Develop the skill and talent of their team
Complete reports	
Maintain safe work environment	

Barriers to Performance Excellence

The Six Principles of Service Excellence is a comprehensive approach to effectively improving the work environment, employee performance and the service experience for your customers, all in one initiative. Reading this book will either validate that your organization is moving in the right direction, or it will provide you with new ideas you hadn't considered for improving service and employee performance. While there are many barriers that impede service excellence within an organization, most of them fall within four categories: Selection, Skill/Knowledge, Work Environment, and Reward and Recognition.

- **Selection** - Do you select new employees for your organization, not only based on their technical ability, but, also, based on their ability to support and energize the philosophical values of your organization?

- **Skill / Knowledge** - Do you integrate the organizational vision, mission, business objectives and service standards into every aspect of employee training and development?

- **Work Environment** - Do you ensure your team has the most effective processes, systems and tools in place to support service excellence? Do your employees feel knowledgeable and empowered to take care of customer problems?

- **Reward and Recognition** - Do you reward and recognize employees based on their consistent demonstration of your philosophical values?

If you answered *no* to any of these questions, we suggest you dig deeper to determine the root cause of these barriers. In Chapter Six, we further explore how to overcome barriers that are preventing organizations from excelling by walking you through the service excellence gap analysis process.

The Role of Employee Empowerment

Employee empowerment, along with alignment, consistency, and teamwork, are key contributors to creating a culture of service excellence. Empowerment is a word that is frequently misused and misunderstood. So what is empowerment? *It is letting go and giving your employees the freedom to do their job the best way they can, after you have trained them.* At The Ritz-Carlton, every employee is empowered up to $2,000 to resolve a customer opportunity (problem) or to delight a customer without seeking the authority of a manager. I consider this the ultimate example of employee empowerment, and I know first hand that, because of the level of customer problem resolution training The Ritz-Carlton employees receive, it is extremely rare for a customer opportunity to cost more than a few dollars.

Many organizations I work with aspire to empower their employees, but are afraid to allow them to make even *minor* decisions to resolve customer complaints without a manager's involvement. This creates an unhealthy environment in which employees lack the initiative or independent will to make *any* decisions (good or bad), for fear of reprisal. We have all experienced those "moments of truth," when an employee's inability to make a simple decision has been detrimental to both the company and the customer.

Employee empowerment does not occur by chance. It is an element of the work environment that is developed, over time, by leaders and based on trust. To understand the essence of employee empowerment, we must understand that:

- **Empowerment Is** – a process, a journey, a set of conditions. It is built on trust and is about people. While empowerment may be risky for the leader, it is extremely liberating for the employee.

- **Empowerment Is Not** – manipulating or abandoning people to do the job the best way they can without direction or guidance. It is not about dumping a boat load of responsibilities on employees who have been provided no leadership. Ultimately, empowerment is not something that can be given away, it must be earned.

To effectively empower employees, you must first identify the top ten chronic customer problems employees regularly encounter and the chronic internal problems that cause defects, frustration and rework in the workplace. I cannot tell you how many leaders I talk to regularly who have no idea what the top ten chronic customer problems are within their organizations. They have never asked for or sought out the information. Next, you must develop processes for resolving those chronic problems, implement the processes, and hold employees accountable for delivering excellence every day. There is no other way to combat mediocre service. Simply stated, you should do your homework before you start empowering employees.

Key Points

- In order to truly appreciate *The Six Principles of Service Excellence,* leaders must be consumed with the pursuit of excellence.

- Mediocre organizations merely strive to attain customer satisfaction, while exceptional organizations aspire to go above and beyond in order to develop a loyal customer following.

- Employees who focus on both the function and *purpose* of their work find meaning in their job. Their mindset extends beyond *just* being a waiter, housekeeper or cashier. They see themselves as service professionals and, therefore, willingly go above and beyond to take care of the customer.

- Employee empowerment does not occur overnight or by chance. It is an element of the work environment that is developed over time and based on mutual trust.

—◈—

CREATING THE BASIS
FOR THE CULTURE
Part 1

The Six Principles of
Service Excellence™

Vision/Mission **Business Goals** **Service Standards**	**Part I** **CREATING THE BASIS FOR THE CULTURE**
Intervention Selection Learning Strategy Organizational Alignment	Part II CREATING THE BASIS FOR SUSTAINABILITY
Measurement Leadership Accountability	Part III CREATING THE BASIS FOR CREDIBILITY
Role of the Leader Personal Application	Part IV TOOLS TO DRIVE SERVICE EXCELLENCE

Let's Get Started

After reading Chapters One and Two, you should begin to realize that creating a culture of service excellence is attainable. It is not a daunting task and can be done at the organizational or work team level with the right commitment from leadership. As you begin to evaluate the effectiveness of your current vision and mission statements, business objectives, and service standards, I will guide you through a process to determine their effectiveness.

This may lead you to consider rewriting your organization's service philosophy (vision, mission, and service standards). If your organization does not have these foundational elements in place, I will also guide you through the process of creating a service philosophy that all personnel can embrace and consistently demonstrate in their behaviors.

— ◈ —

VISION and MISSION
Chapter 3

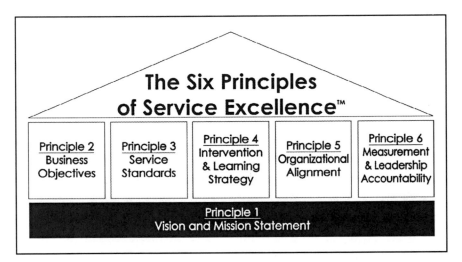

The Six Principles
of Service Excellence™

| Principle 2 Business Objectives | Principle 3 Service Standards | Principle 4 Intervention & Learning Strategy | Principle 5 Organizational Alignment | Principle 6 Measurement & Leadership Accountability |

Principle 1
Vision and Mission Statement

Service is a choice! To fully engage employees to make the choice to deliver exceptional service consistently, they must find an emotional connection with the organizational vision and mission. You must fully engage their hearts, minds, bodies, and souls.

Connecting with the Vision and Mission

Earlier I noted that Performance Solutions by Design conducted a comprehensive study of the organizations with which we consulted during a twelve month period and uncovered astounding data.

- 91% of the organizations in the study had no vision statement.

- 88% of the organizations examined had a mission statement. However, after conducting an in-depth gap analysis, 66% found that their mission statements were no longer relevant, in relation to their elevated service expectations.

With staggering statistics such as these, it is easy to understand why most organizations fail to fully engage employees to consistently deliver superior customer service.

Many organizations have either a vision or a mission statement. Such proclamations have become fairly standard decoration for company bulletin boards, office corridors, executive conference rooms, and annual reports. But, without digging up a copy, can you honestly recite your company's vision statement and mission statement? What percentage of your employees can tell you what they are? Let's say you and your employees can actually recite the mission and vision statements; however, do you and they believe them? In other words, are these statements really taken seriously?

At a floundering transportation company where the vision and mission statement are not taken seriously, I once asked an employee to tell me about her company's vision statement. She quickly responded: *"To hold things together long enough for the new CEO to amass a humongous retirement package."*

That is not, of course, what it says on the company's bulletin boards or in its annual report; however, I suspect that the employee's bitter interpretation is closer to the truth than the lofty goals the company purports to pursue. And, its declining stock value seems to support my suspicions.

The Purpose of Vision and Mission Statements

It is a great temptation to include in this chapter a collection of the most poorly conceived vision and mission statements I have come across. Since that would be unkind, let's examine the purpose and function of vision and mission statements in order to help you assess the effectiveness of yours.

We established, in Chapter One, that creating a culture of service excellence cannot be accomplished without fully engaged leaders and employees who are aligned with and motivated by the vision and mission of the organization. Being aligned and engaged helps each individual, in turn, understand his or her individual role, contribution, and purpose in positively affecting service excellence daily. The true purpose of a vision and mission statement is not just to be attractively framed and mounted on the walls of your office or facility; it is to help employees emotionally connect with the purpose of their work and how that purpose relates to the overall success of the company.

When you look at The Six Principles model, clearly the vision and mission of an organization are the foundation for creating the culture. This is why it is critical that you select or hire employees, from the CEO to the janitor, who naturally align with, respect and support the organization's vision and mission. Once you have the right people in place and provide them the proper skills, knowledge, and a work environment where service excellence can thrive, they will become self-motivated and make every effort necessary to support a culture of service excellence. All things considered, having well written vision and mission statements that are relevant and actionable helps create clarity.

If your organization already has a vision statement and mission statement, the first step in creating a culture of service excellence is to take a close look at the statements and determine their current relevance to your business objectives. Are they interconnected, or are they contradictory?

Even within organizations that have vision and mission statements, I have found that their statements seldom address what is most important. Many of their executives naively believe that a company's vision and mission play no essential role in driving world-class customer service. Therefore, they do not believe it is important to drive the vision and mission system-wide. While the business objectives of the organization are subject to change through periodic enhancements, the organization's vision and mission should be timeless and written as though they will never change – even though they may slightly evolve as your organization matures. In organizations where the vision and mission are very strong and integrated into the culture, they often drive the successful achievement of business objectives and the strategic direction of the company.

The Copy Center Experience

A few months ago, I visited a well-known copy center to have some rather thick training manuals reproduced. I greeted the young lady at the desk with a smile and explained that I needed five copies of the manual. In disgust, she batted her eyes and quickly pointed me in the direction of what looked like an ATM machine. "You need to go there," she instructed in a stern voice. Not understanding why she was pointing to the machine, I asked her why I needed to go over there. With unconcealed frustration, she told me I needed to get a copy card and put money on it in order to make copies.

Based on the first thirty seconds of my interaction with this employee, my first impression of this national chain was surely not what the CEO would envision or expect, and yet the experience failed to improve. Unfortunately, I had to make my own copies, and, because I did not understand how to operate the copier, it jammed. Consequently, I had to call on the only person available, the same young lady who had apparently gotten up on the wrong side of the bed that day.

Just think of the opportunity she had to change my impression of her company! Instead, she huffed, puffed and reluctantly assisted me, offering no smile or apology for the copier malfunction. Ironically, directly behind her was a huge, framed poster of the company's mission statement, which outlined how important the customer is to the chain. I resisted asking her to turn around and read it.

This experience makes me acutely aware of how often employees are emotionally disengaged from the purpose of their work. It was obvious that the copy center employee had no clue about the devastating magnitude her 15 minute interaction could have on me as a customer. I am also confident that the CEO of this national copy center chain would be appalled by the behavior of this employee. However, similar customer/employee interactions occur countless times every day and in every industry because of disengaged employees who are unable to link the purpose of their work with the importance of customer satisfaction and loyalty.

What Should a Vision Statement Be?

Your vision statement should plainly state what you want to be. It should paint a vivid picture of your desired or future state. Some organizations do not feel it is necessary for them to have both vision and mission statements. While I disagree, if you choose to have only one, perhaps the mission statement is more important. Still, the addition of a good vision statement also helps employees understand what all of you, as an organization, are working to achieve.

A vision statement should be summed up in one brief sentence. Any statement that rambles on needs more work because it is not yet distilled. The Ritz-Carlton's vision statement is four words: *Service and profit dominance.* This clear image helps employees understand what everyone is working so hard to achieve. The vision statement for Performance Solutions by Design is equally direct: *To be the undisputed leader in driving cultural change and performance excellence.* I see both of these as clear vision statements that any employee can easily remember, understand, and work toward.

Listed below are a few questions to consider in assessing the strength, relevance, and effectiveness of your organization's vision statement. If you answer "no" to three or more of the statements, it's time to re-evaluate the relevancy of your organization's vision statement because it is most likely outdated and needs to be rewritten or revised.

- *Our vision statement is discussed regularly by our senior leaders*

- *Our managers and supervisors know the vision of our organization*

- *Our employees know the vision of our organization*

- *Our vision statement is relevant to the job we do every day*

- *All departmental goals are aligned with the company's vision statement*

- *Employees within my department strongly support the company's vision*

What Should a Mission Statement Be?

A well written mission statement consists of a few sentences that define the purpose of the organization and act as a daily self-evaluation for every employee. So, if your organization's mission statement was reworded in the form of questions, could you answer "yes" to all of them? If so, most likely you accomplished excellence that day.

Oddly enough, employees and leaders occasionally confuse the organization's goals and objectives with its mission. To better clarify the difference between organizational goals and an organizational mission statement, consider this example. An organizational goal might be to increase sales by 25 percent during the fiscal year. While that is a worthy goal, it does not define the purpose of the organization. Your mission statement should state how you plan to achieve the goal. To be effectively driven, your organizational mission statement should also be short, concise and easily understood by everyone within the company.

Since I mentioned my company's vision statement, it seems logical to follow it with our mission statement:

> *Performance Solutions by Design is a value-based organization that is authentic and unconventional in its approach.*
>
> *We believe that our talents, uniqueness, and diversity contribute to our effectiveness in seeking to discover and reawaken the fire within the organizations with whom we work.*
>
> *In an honest and supportive environment, we strive to maintain balance in our lives and create fulfillment in our work.*

Creating an Effective Mission Statement

The Six Principles of Service Excellence process starts with vision and mission because the aspirations and purpose of your organization drive everything. Whether you already have a mission statement or are considering what one for your organization should say, there are five steps in determining the relevance and effectiveness of your mission statement in driving service excellence. They are: *Assess, Revise or Rewrite, Stakeholder Feedback, Finalize, and Align.* Let's tackle these five steps one at a time, which will make the logic of the approach apparent.

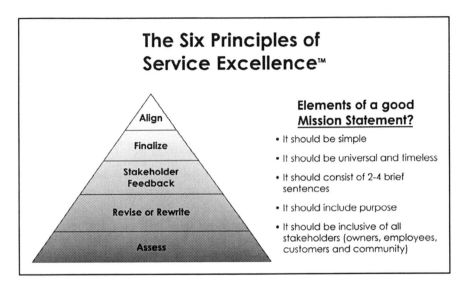

The Six Principles of Service Excellence™

Align

Finalize

Stakeholder Feedback

Revise or Rewrite

Assess

Elements of a good Mission Statement?

• It should be simple

• It should be universal and timeless

• It should consist of 2-4 brief sentences

• It should include purpose

• It should be inclusive of all stakeholders (owners, employees, customers and community)

Step 1: Assess - In assessing the relevance of your organization's mission, the questions you might ask key stakeholders include:

• *Is the mission clearly understood by all?*

• *Is it realistic and actionable?*

• *Is there an effective process in place for sustaining it?*

• *Is it still applicable or relevant today?*

• *Is the organization's direction interconnected or contradictory to the stated mission?*

• *Are our customer service practices aligned with the mission?*

• *Does the mission address our commitment to service excellence?*

Step 2: Revise or Rewrite - Based on the feedback from your key stakeholders, a critical decision must be made as to whether your organization's (division's or department's) mission statement is fine as is, should be revised, or needs to be totally rewritten. Organizations that are the most successful at driving service excellence work very hard to develop their culture around relevant vision and mission statements that spell out their commitment to service excellence. In forming their statements, they consciously or unconsciously address these questions:

- *What do we want to **have, do** or **be** as an organization?*
- *What **legacy** do we want to leave behind?*
- *What will **success** look like for us as an organization in ten years?*
- *How will we know when we have **arrived**?*
- *If we were the **undisputed leaders** in our industry, what would our competitors, employees, customers, and the media be saying about us?*

Step 3: Stakeholder Feedback - One hundred percent buy-in and support from all stakeholders is critical to moving your organization's mission statement from just words printed on a piece of paper to an inspiring statement by which everyone judges his or her contribution to the organization. To ensure there is support and buy-in for your new or existing service excellence initiative, it's important that all stakeholders have an opportunity to review and give honest feedback prior to a new mission statement being finalized. This will ensure having a document everyone can live by. The process also creates a sense of ownership of the mission and a sense of obligation to achieving it.

To make this happen, your leadership team or an appointed service excellence team will need to determine the most effective method of getting stakeholder feedback. Whether it is through group meetings, email correspondence, or printed copies distributed personally or by interoffice mail, the important thing is to ask for input. Those who are comfortable with the first statement submitted often won't reply, while those who have objections or thoughts to add usually reply immediately. Still, a ten percent response is about what you should expect. What's important is including the stakeholders in the process and giving each one an opportunity to participate. This simple action will greatly increase the number of employees who buy-in and consciously work toward living up to the statement.

Step 4: Finalize - Once all interested stakeholders have had their say, it's time to finalize the new mission statement. This is sometimes a painful – but necessary – process because of the wordsmithing needed. However, once the document is finalized, it is truly powerful and a statement that everyone can live with, be proud to represent, and consistently energize.

Step 5: Align - It is hard to perceive a truly *functional, effective* and *successful* organization that is not intricately connected to a vision and mission. Once the vision and mission are finalized, all leaders within the organization must be held to the highest level of accountability for enlivening it in their departments and divisions. Leaders' ultimate roles are to ensure that all employees emotionally connect with the vision and mission of the organization, live it every day, and understand their individual contributes to the success of the organization.

Benefits of a Mission Statement

The process of writing a mission statement forces us to define and clarify who we are by asking: What is our purpose? What is important to us? What qualities or characteristics would we like to demonstrate? What legacy do we want to leave?

Recently, I worked with a large, prominent law firm that has more than a century of tradition. However, it was not until they started the service excellence journey that they realized the importance and value of clarifying their mission statement in order to take service within their organization to a higher level. Breaking with more than a century of tradition was a very tough decision for them to make. However, the CEO purposefully engaged a team of fifteen dynamic employees across several departments to rewrite the mission statement. The benefit for them is a highly charged workforce, where 100% of the employees now understand the aspirations of the firm, know their individual purpose, and feel they are valued contributors in achieving service excellence.

What Powers a Successful Vision and Mission?

In a word, the answer is leadership. Leadership must be the living role model of the mission and philosophical values for which an organization stands. All leaders, from senior leadership through supervisors, must be held accountable for knowing, owning, and energizing the vision and mission of the organization. You have to live your vision and mission daily, if you expect the people who look to you for direction to live them.

Both vision and mission should be discussed and repeated as regularly as leadership talks about productivity, financial goals, and objectives such as sales, revenue, and profits. Not until leadership is repetitious in articulating its understanding and expectations concerning the organization's vision and mission, will these philosophical values become reality in the minds of your employees. Once your people clearly understand the vision and mission, they begin emotionally connecting with them, mind, heart, and soul. It is at this point that you begin seeing your philosophical values swell the bottom line.

A common pitfall in driving organizational vision and mission is thinking this type stuff is only for the front-line employees. Leaders often want to start by reinforcing the service culture and philosophical values at the bottom with line employees, hoping it will eventually trickle up. This "trickle up" mentality is what causes dysfunctional service within organizations. A culture of hypocrisy is created when leaders expect employees to behave in ways that are not consistently exemplified by the leaders themselves. When leadership fails to hold itself accountable for driving the mission and vision of the organization, service excellence can be neither achieved nor sustained because the leaders are the people who most need to understand the culture and philosophy; however, they are not regularly exposed to it.

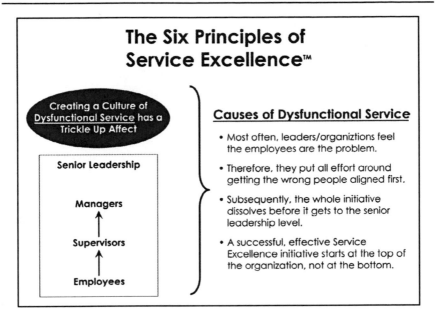

The Six Principles of
Service Excellence™

Creating a Culture of
Dysfunctional Service has a
Trickle Up Affect

Senior Leadership

Managers

Supervisors

Employees

Causes of Dysfunctional Service

• Most often, leaders/organiztions feel the employees are the problem.

• Therefore, they put all effort around getting the wrong people aligned first.

• Subsequently, the whole initiative dissolves before it gets to the senior leadership level.

• A successful, effective Service Excellence initiative starts at the top of the organization, not at the bottom.

The Mission Statement Test

If you decide to rewrite or revise your organizational mission statement based on what you have learned in this chapter, here is a quick and easy way to assess the effectiveness of your new mission statement. Ask yourself and the stakeholders:

- *Does our new mission statement support our vision?*

- *Does our new mission statement assert our unique philosophy of doing business?*

- *Can our new mission statement be used to evaluate work performance?*

- *Can our new mission statement be embraced by everyone throughout the organization?*

When you can answer *yes* to all the above, you have a mission statement that can guide your organization to amazing accomplishments.

Key Points

- Service excellence cannot be accomplished without employees being fully aligned, motivated by and engaged with the vision and mission of the organization.

- The first step in creating a culture of service excellence is taking a close look at the organization's vision and mission to determine their current relevance in achieving the business goals. Well written mission statements define, articulate, and clarify the purpose of the organization.

- It also takes everyone moving in the same direction to drive the vision and mission. In the words of one of my most trusted mentors, Horst Schulze, everyone must: *CONNECT* emotionally with the mission/vision; *COMMIT* to living it every day; *INITIATE* an action plan to make things happen; *FOCUS* on the goal of service excellence; and *ENERGIZE* the mission/vision daily.

BUSINESS OBJECTIVES
Chapter 4

The Six Principles
of Service Excellence™

| Principle 2 Business Objectives | Principle 3 Service Standards | Principle 4 Intervention & Learning Strategy | Principle 5 Organizational Alignment | Principle 6 Measurement & Leadership Accountability |

Principle 1
Vision and Mission Statement

This chapter is not about how to write effective business objectives. It's about ensuring that your organizational objectives incorporate goals relative to achieving service excellence. If you suffer a shortage of loyal customers and have difficulty retaining loyal employees, those conditions make it extremely difficult to achieve profitability, market share, growth, and expansion goals. As elementary as that sounds, in most organizations business objectives rarely include goals relative to customer loyalty, employee loyalty, employee retention, and defect elimination, which are all important in reaching financial success.

What are the business objectives of your organization? If you know them, these objectives should be clearly articulated throughout the organization to the extent that all employees not only understand them, they are also clear about their individual roles in accomplishing them.

Business' Biggest Shortcoming

In many organizations, strategic alignment is the biggest business shortcoming. Without strategic alignment, you are unable to create a work environment where employees not only understand the goals, but also emotionally connect with them and have a strong desire to help achieve or even exceed the goals. My observation is that most business objectives and strategic plans are developed in the boardroom; sadly, they seldom leave the confines of those four walls. Based on the service excellence study conducted by Performance Solutions by Design, we found 100 percent of the companies polled have business objectives. However, only 22 percent share their business objectives with all their employees. Therefore, when employees report to work each day, they are not only disengaged with the vision and mission of the organization, they also have no clue as to what the vitally important goals or objectives are.

I liken this to trying to find your way out of a jungle without a map or compass. Therefore, it is important to review your organization's current business objectives and strategic plan with everyone in the organization. Then, assess leadership's ability to clarify and articulate them departmentally. And finally, ensure specific measures are in place to quantify what success or achievement of these goals will look like.

Assessment of Business Objectives

When assessing the affect your organization's business objectives have on improving service excellence, ask the following:

- **Do we have business objectives that address service excellence?** Acceptable examples include: Increase Customer Loyalty; Increase Employee Loyalty; Reduce Employee accountable for incorporating one or two service excellence objectives in its strategic plan.

If you answered no to the first two questions, most likely your organizational or departmental business objectives need to be broadened to also address service improvement goals and expectation.

Effective Business Objectives

We have spent considerable time focusing on what constitutes ineffective or incomplete business objectives. Now let's look at what contributes to developing effective business objectives. As previously established, they must also be *realistic, measurable,* and *quantifiable.* Business objectives should be *accomplishment based* and focus on output, rather than behaviors. And most importantly, they must be *timeline centered* so employees know when this business objective is expected to be achieved (within one year, five years, or ten years).

Here are a few examples of good service excellence business objectives:

- 20% Increase in Employee Retention
- 25% Increase in Employee Satisfaction/Loyalty
- 10% Increase in Customer Satisfaction/Loyalty
- 30% Reduction in Service/Product Defects
- 30% Reduction in Customer Complaints

These business objectives take into consideration that your organization has already developed equally important financial and market-driven business objectives. You might ask yourself: What makes service excellence goals so important? Well, we know that no organization can sustain long-term financial success without high employee retention. We also know that high employee retention is a by-product of a work environment that fosters high employee satisfaction and subsequent employee loyalty. The same cycle is evident when we focus on reducing customer problems or service defects. The result becomes fewer customer complaints and,

Turnover; Reduce Customer Problems or Complaints; Increase Quality of Service and Products Delivered.

- **Are our service-oriented business objectives realistic?** This is really a double question. First, are the current objectives realistic in the eyes of *management*? Second, are they realistic in the eyes of *all others down the organizational ladder*? If every level does not believe a goal is realistic, the chances of it being achieved are nonexistent.

- **Are they actionable?** Vague business objectives are often not actionable; they must be clarified with real life examples for the employee. If the business objective is to increase customer loyalty, an action that would contribute to achieving that would be consistently using the customer's name and remembering something special about the customer in order to make every interaction exceptional.

- **Are they quantifiable?** It's not enough to just draft five or six business objectives and call it a day. Prior to announcing a goal, you should know how to measure its results. Moreover, employees need to know they have been assigned a quantifiable goal. For example, hotel employees might be challenged to increase customer loyalty by 20 percent, while airline employees might be set a goal of reducing passenger lost luggage by 60 percent. Goals that can be numerically measured eventually show employees how successful they have or have not been.

- **Are they communicated system-wide?** Your business objectives should be given special emphasis, if you expect to achieve them. Certainly you should make use of all your existing communication channels: the employee newsletter, emails, bulletin boards and departmental or team meetings.

- **Are they part of every department's strategic plan?** We have said it before: Business objectives involving service excellence are not just the domain of the front line employees who directly interact with customers. Whether there is direct customer contact or not, every department should be overtime, higher customer satisfaction, and, most importantly, high customer loyalty.

This is not rocket science. In a nutshell, if you do not include service excellence goals in your business objectives, performance expectations of your employees will never become a strategic focus; consequently, the quality of customer service will never improve.

The Impact of Business Objectives on Customer Loyalty

I am a long-time customer of my bank. Their service is accurate, fast, friendly and consistent. However, the local branch that I use is truly outstanding. A couple of times a month, I make transactions at their drive-through window, where the same two tellers are always posted. Without fail, I receive a warm and friendly greeting. Each teller always uses my name and asks if there is anything else she can assist me with. Every transaction concludes with thanking me for the business and saying they hope they have served me with excellence. Both tellers are truly engaged and clearly find purpose and meaning in their work; consequently, they deliver a formidable contribution to attaining the bank's goals.

Recently, I took the time to go inside to meet the branch manager and praise these ladies. If the banking industry could clone them, few customers would be lured by incentives such as free checking and other complimentary services offered by the competition.

Training's Role

No service excellence initiative should be solely supported by a training and development department. The initiative should be a company-wide effort that also involves operations, human resources, quality, finance, sales and marketing, et cetera. A service excellence initiative that is backed by effective business objectives helps those administering training to determine what skills and knowledge are necessary to support the workforce in the successful achievement of the goal.

Training's real role is to help leadership identify and close the skill and knowledge gaps that prevent teams from performing consistently at an optimal level. Dysfunction often occurs when training is relegated to creating fun – yet ineffective – training workshops that have no immediate impact on the business drivers of the organization. In identifying service and performance gaps, trainers must be willing to acknowledge that the barriers to superior performance are sometimes more than training. Operational process improvement and quality initiatives are also sometimes barriers. A keen training professional never starts a service excellence initiative or creates a customer service class without first understanding what business drivers or objectives are at stake and what their effectiveness will be judged against.

Repetition Is Good

Repetition is the most effective way to ensure the service excellence business objectives are understood and energized by all. The more you talk about them, the more evident they become within your organization's everyday life. When I worked for The Ritz-Carlton, every employee was responsible for knowing the organization's business objectives. From the general manager to the dishwasher, no one was exempt. The business objectives were so vitally important to the success of the organization that a service standard about the business objectives was created, so that everyone would remember them and their responsibility to support them.

Go beyond displaying your vision and mission statements throughout the organization; also, display your organization's business objectives. At every possible opportunity, point out the connection between them. Furthermore, in order to prevent them from becoming just posters on the wall, discuss and evaluate them regularly. Every employee within the organization should be able to express in words what his or her contributions are to the service excellence initiative. This ensures that their hearts and souls are involved and that the leader is keeping the business objectives before them every day.

Each department, division, or business unit should have individual objectives or goals that are completely aligned with the big picture.

If the organization, as a whole, is focused on increased employee retention, increased customer loyalty, and defect elimination, these objectives should also be evident and evaluated at the work team level. Otherwise, the objectives will have no relevance or positive affect at the work team level, thus severely limiting the organization's ability to improve and succeed.

Accomplishment-based Objectives

As I mentioned earlier in this chapter, the most effective service excellence business objectives are accomplishment oriented and not behavior oriented. Accomplishment validates the focus on realistic, quantifiable measurements because it is not based on improved employee or customer behavior.

Behavior Based Business Objectives	Accomplishment Based Business Objectives
• *We will increase teamwork* • *We will have happier employees* • *We will have happier customers* • *We will enjoy coming to work* • *We will make more revenue this year*	• *Increase Revenue and Profit by 8%* • *Decrease Rework by 25%* • *Decrease Cycle Time by 25%* • *Reduce Employee Turnover by 10%* • *Increase Customer Satisfaction or Loyalty by 10%* • *Increase Employee Satisfaction or Loyalty by 10%*

Behavior based goals are least effective. They include goals such as having happier employees, happier customers, and better work processes. Without quantifiable measures, these goals may be perceived as subjective, unfocused, and baseless. So, set up a system of measurements, and your people will measure up.

Key Points

- Focusing on business objectives ensures that any service excellence initiative is strategically aligned with key business priorities. It also ensures the success of your service excellence initiative, based on expected accomplishments (or outcomes), not solely on employee behaviors.

- Clearly defined business objectives ensure the service excellence initiative is not solely based on training and development workshops and seminars. While each, of course, has its place in the grand scheme of things, focusing on business objectives ensures every departmental and divisional level is actively involved in the implementation and support of your service excellence initiative.

—◈—

SERVICE STANDARDS
Chapter 5

The Six Principles
of Service Excellence™

Principle 2 Business Objectives	Principle 3 Service Standards	Principle 4 Intervention & Learning Strategy	Principle 5 Organizational Alignment	Principle 6 Measurement & Leadership Accountability

Principle 1
Vision and Mission Statement

To achieve service excellence, employees must understand exactly what they are expected to do. They need to know what specific behaviors you expect them to consistently demonstrate and exemplify.

Time after time in the previous chapters, we focused on the importance of a well defined service philosophy that includes vision and mission statements and business objectives. We also elaborated on the value of everyone in the workforce being held individually accountable for knowing, owning and energizing these philosophical values of the organization. Also, we established that excellence cannot be achieved without alignment, consistency, accountability, teamwork and empowerment. Now, we focus on the importance of service standards, those *uncompromising* behaviors or actions that, when consistently exemplified by everyone from the CEO to the custodian, deliver an exceptional service experience to every customer.

Never Assume Anything When It Comes to Service

Imagine an organization with a clearly defined mission and vision – but no guiding principles to help employees connect or understand how to energize them. Sadly, this is an everyday reality in many organizations because their leaders do not see the need for service standards. Apparently, such leaders assume that, because the vision and mission statements are posted in every nook and cranny throughout the office or facility, employees know what they need to do to live them. However, *assumption is not always a good thing* – especially when it affects customer service.

A service excellence study conducted by *Performance Solutions by Design* found that only 22 percent of the organizations polled have relevant service standards. Unfortunately, most organizations confuse service standards with brand standards.

Service Standards versus Brand Standards

Earlier, I mentioned that service standards sometimes become confused with brand standards; however, the two are quite different. Service standards are a set of core covenants or ground rules that are mutually agreed upon and articulate exactly *what is expected of every employee* in pursuit of the mission, vision and business objectives. Service standards focus on the emotional aspects of the customer experience.

On the other hand, brand standards typically articulate the *physical aspects* of the customer experience. They can be summed up as those physical, environmental, or functional standards that are mutually agreed upon and are consistent throughout an organization.

Examples of Service Standards	Examples of Brand Standards
• Proper telephone etiquette is used by everyone. We always answer within three rings and with a smile. • We work to promote a positive work environment, and are courteous and respectful to everyone. • We foster a work environment that empowers and encourages everyone to take initiative. • If a complaint arises, we respond with a sense of urgency. We listen attentively, offer a genuine apology, solve the problem, and thank the customer for providing us with the opportunity to improve. • Everyone is responsible for conveying a professional image. We always wear our name tags, dress conservatively, and consistently adhere to the grooming standards concerning hair, jewelry, make-up, and uniforms. • We lead by example. We always take the initiative to make things better in our work environment and always express concerns to the person who can resolve them.	• Directional signage is present, visible, and adequate in all guest contact areas throughout the facility. Signage is granite – not wood or plastic – and uniform throughout the facility. • All landscape areas are maintained in excellent condition. Flower beds are freshly mulched and weed-free. Bushes and hedges are kept neatly trimmed. • Parking areas are free of major cracks. No chips or faded paint on striping or curbing. No potholes. • Flags displayed are not worn, faded, or frayed. • All public areas are free of dust, cobwebs, debris, and visible stains. • Restrooms/locker rooms are properly supply stocked with paper products and additional supplies. Amenities work properly. Stock levels of soap, towels and other amenities are replenished when ¾ full.
SERVICE STANDARDS ensure consistency in the **emotional aspects** of the customer experience.	**BRAND STANDARDS** ensure consistency in the **functional or physical aspects** of the customer experience.
Both Brand Standard and Service Standards are extremely important!	

The purpose of service standards is to literally spell out how employees are expected to act or behave in support of the organization's service culture and philosophical values. Service standards leave no room for leadership assumption or individual employee interpretation; they are created to hold everyone throughout the organization accountable to the highest levels of customer service.

A common shortcoming in business is to create service standards that apply only to line staff or administrative employees, yet require no behavior changes or accountability from leadership. For some reason, leaders always want to fix everyone else. Service standards are created to be known, owned, and energized by all employees at all levels. Your service standards should be written or created with the goal of enabling *every* employee within the organization to excel.

I know some of you are thinking this is silly, simple stuff. The interesting thing about service standards is that they are common sense; they are things that most employees naturally know they should do but often don't. Employees know that they should use proper company verbiage when addressing customers; they know that they should always greet the customer with a smile; they know that the telephone should be answered quickly; they know that safety is a priority within the company…and so forth. However, in pursuit of service excellence, you cannot truly hold employees accountable if these standards are never placed in writing, regularly discussed, and exemplified by leadership on a regular basis.

A Small Doctor's Office

Service excellence is often best demonstrated in small work environments where there is no threat of bureaucracy and its layers of management. A year ago, I had a medical condition that required immediate surgery. Prior to surgery, I had an MRI which was read by my radiologist.

My radiologist has a small staff of about six people. From the time you walk into his office's lobby until you leave, you are taken care of; you feel a high sense of confidence that you are in very capable hands. I can easily contrast my radiologist's office to other medical facilities where you are coldly greeted, demanded to fill out paperwork, and then herded off to a small examining room to wait 40-to-60 minutes before seeing a physician. However, at my radiologist's office, the receptionist warmly greets you and kindly asks for your insurance information, before you are seated. In the event of a wait, she lets you know immediately and asks if you would prefer to reschedule your visit. When a follow-up visit is required, she finds a date that fits your schedule and the doctor's. If you have visited the office more than a few times, the staff knows and uses your name. They understand that patients can sometimes be irritable, and they willingly compensate for that.

I believe the support staff in this office is exceptional because they work for an exceptional leader. My radiologist exemplifies service excellence as he warmly greets you and escorts you to his office. He does not rush you through the consultation, carefully ensuring that you understand every aspect of your condition and all alternatives before you leave. Additional sources of information are offered so that you can better understand your condition. Most of your questions are answered before you leave, and if you have additional questions later, he is always open to a telephone call to provide clarification. I am a loyal patient and rave about him to everyone as an example of what good physician care is all about.

Doctors have many issues to deal with every day. It is comforting when you find a physician who is not only a subject matter expert – that's expected – but also understands the importance of ensuring that every patient is satisfied with the service provided. When I recently switched to another medical insurance company, one of my major determining factors was if my radiologist and my primary care physician were on their list of approved physicians. I wouldn't trust my health to anyone else. That's what customer loyalty in healthcare is all about.

These physicians do an outstanding job of exemplifying what service excellence is for their employees. They are real life examples of leaders who not only take their profession seriously, but also take service seriously. Exemplifying the service standards of your organization means the leader must know, understand, communicate, and demonstrate service excellence every day.

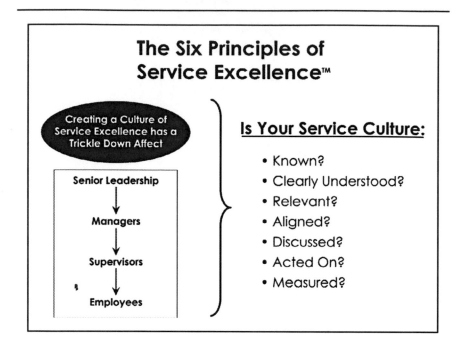

The Six Principles of Service Excellence™

Creating a Culture of Service Excellence has a Trickle Down Affect

Senior Leadership

↓

Managers

↓

Supervisors

↓

Employees

Is Your Service Culture:

- Known?
- Clearly Understood?
- Relevant?
- Aligned?
- Discussed?
- Acted On?
- Measured?

Assessing Relevance and Effectiveness

If your organization currently has service standards, here are a few questions to help you quickly assess their relevancy and effectiveness:

- *Are our service standards known and embraced by every employee at every level?*

- *Are our service standards clearly understood by every employee at every level?*

- *Are our service standards still relevant, or do they need updating?*

- *Is every department aligned with the service standards?*

- *Do our leaders discuss the service standards on a regular basis?*

- *Are the service standards a part of every employee's daily routine?*

- *Do we measure our employees' ability to energize the service standards?*

- *Do our service standards incorporate the things employees need to do to bring our vision, mission, and business objectives to life?*

- *Are our service standards incorporated in the New Employee Orientation and other training programs?*

- *How do we hold employees accountable for upholding the service standards?*

- *Are there any service standards that should be added or deleted?*

If you currently have service standards but answered *no* to three or more of the above questions, I recommend you react quickly. There are issues that may be hindering your ability to attract and retain highly engaged employees, loyal customers, and profits.

Start with Employee Aspirations

If you have decided to create or revise your organization's service standards, the most effective approach is to think about all of the things that you *aspire* to have your employees do. What are those things that, if consistently exemplified, would embrace the definition of service excellence for your organization?

Too often we focus on the bad things employees do, those behaviors that cause them to deliver poor customer service. To jump start the process of developing effective service standards, I suggest you focus on five or six positive behaviors to which you aspire. Again, considering those things that, if your employees do without fail, will set your organization's level of service apart from the competition's.

Employee Aspirations (Desired Behaviors)

To consistently follow grooming and appearance standards

To greet every customer with a warm and friendly smile

To answer the telephone promptly and with finesse

To resolve customer problems quickly and effectively

To practice teamwork and creative collaboration

To be empowered to identify ways to improve the work environment

---

Involving Employees in Creating Service Standards

Involving employees and leaders in the creation of service standards ensures support and buy-in at all levels. Here are a few suggestions for maximizing employee involvement:

- **Cross-Functional Team:** The process is similar to the development of your mission and vision statements. Select a small cross-section of exemplary employees and leaders from various departments within your organization. Challenge them with the task of drafting 10-to-15 service standards for the organization. Allow them at least a half-day meeting to develop the draft. This meeting should be facilitated by a nonbiased leader who is capable of clearly expressing the organization's vision, mission, and business objectives so that the team and the service standards they create are aligned with the philosophical values. I recommend having the leader start the process by identifying the *employee aspirations* of the organization.

- **Senior Leadership Involvement:** Someone from the cross-functional team should be designated to meet with senior leadership, distribute copies of the drafted service standards, and lead a discussion of the process and rationale behind the drafted standards. Senior leadership is allowed to make suggestions, but should do so in a manner that will not stifle the efforts of the cross-functional team. This allows senior leadership to determine if there are any service gaps its members would like included and, therefore, make positive recommendations.

- **All Employee Feedback:** The cross-functional team should refine the drafted service standards, based on feedback from senior leadership. Next the information should be distributed to every employee. Furthermore, this should be done in a creative, non-threatening manner, such as a contest that recognizes and awards the first ten responses with fun prizes. The purpose of sharing the draft is to make everyone aware of the new service standards, why you are implementing or enhancing them, and get their buy-in. Expect to get a 5-to-10 percent response rate, as most employees will not respond; however, they appreciate being asked their opinion. If high trust exists within your organization, you will receive a higher employee response rate – perhaps as much as 50-to-60 percent. While we have seen great success from the contest suggested above, we also recommend using departmental meetings as a forum for receiving meaningful feedback in a more structured manner.

Using Service Standards Benchmarks

To get the cross-functional team moving in the right direction, provide the team members with the employee aspirations and other company benchmarks or examples of great service standards. Consider reviewing the service standards of organizations that are highly regarded for their customer service. Here are a few examples of great standards from a variety of exceptional organizations with which I have worked:

1. *We are all responsible for living our mission statement. It reaffirms our purpose and service commitment as service professionals towards each other, our patients and community.*

2. *If a complaint arises, listen attentively, offer a genuine apology, solve the problem, and thank the customer for providing us with the opportunity to improve.*

3. *Never lose a customer. Instant customer pacification is the responsibility of every employee. Whoever receives a customer complaint will own it, resolve it to the customer's satisfaction, and record it.*

4. *We personalize the service experience by using the customer's name if and when possible. We acknowledge our repeat and loyal customers by anticipating their preferences and special requests, and fulfilling them.*

5. *Every employee is responsible for improving the work environment; if you are unhappy with a situation within your*

department, address it with the proper individual(s) as soon as possible to resolve the issue.

6. *Remember: our customers are Number One. Always make it your priority to be attentive to their needs.*

7. *We are service professionals; therefore, we make commitments with care and always do what we say we are going to do.*

8. *We convey professionalism by using verbiage that enhances the service experience. We substitute more common and familiar words and phrases, such as "hello" and "no problem," with "good morning/afternoon" and "I will be happy to." We always greet our guests by using Mr., Ms., or Mrs. with their last name.*

9. *We are all sales professionals, regardless of our position. Good selling is good service. We are knowledgeable and aware of all company services, locations and products.*

10. *Everyone is responsible for conveying a professional image. We always wear our name tags, dress conservatively and consistently adhere to our grooming standards concerning hair, jewelry, make-up, uniforms, and footwear.*

If you refer to what was stated earlier concerning employee aspirations, those behaviors that we aspire for all employees to consistently demonstrate, you will see many of them outlined in the service standard examples above. Ultimately, it is most important for your cross-function team to understand that service standards should be clear, concise, simple to understand and easy to remember. I cannot repeat enough that your standards must be communicated at all levels from senior executives to mid-managers, to floor supervisors, to the line level employees responsible for embracing the standards in their daily work.

Developing Effective Service Standards

Just as developing a compelling mission statement is not a simple, one-hour process, developing service standards also takes time and patience. As I mentioned earlier, the most effective service standards are those that are developed using the feedback from the entire workforce. Involving employees in the development of organizational service standards is also a great way to gain their buy-in, support, and commitment. Here are some additional tips to consider in developing effective service standards:

1. **Service Pet Peeves:** Consider all of the pet peeves, the negative things that employees currently do that impede service excellence. Jot them down on a flipchart. Also, consider all of the things your competitors do that frustrate the customer and how you could do them better. *Only consider them as service standards if you are committed to ensuring that your competitors' shortcomings do not become habit in your work environment.*

2. **Limit the Number of Standards:** If written service standards are new to your organization, we suggest narrowing your list to a maximum of ten to fifteen. Initially starting with too many service standards is a perfect recipe for failure.

3. **Don't Get Bogged Down in the Details:** Keep the statements brief, simple, and light. Consider using your existing training programs or a service excellence workshop to cover the details.

4. **Benchmark Other Companies:** Study world-class organizations to get an idea of how they developed, communicate, and sustain their service standards.

5. **Highly Regard Employee Feedback:** Make sure a draft of the service standards is made available to the entire workforce for review and feedback. Remember, 100 percent support and endorsement can only be achieved if everyone has the opportunity to be involved in the process.

6. **Highly Regard Employee Involvement:** Assign a cross-functional team of employees and leaders to finalize the service standards and communicate them to the workforce in a fun and informative manner.

7. **Positively Communicate New Service Standards:** Be extremely careful not to communicate new service standards

in a manner that could be negatively construed. While your service standards are uncompromising behaviors that are expected of everyone, employees should not see them as punitive. Service standards should be communicated in a fun, creative manner that makes all employees proud to have been a part of the development process and makes them eager and willing to comply. At The Ritz-Carlton, we updated the company service standards every four or five years. We often held a contest and recognized those employees who submitted the cleverest, fun clues to help everyone remember the new service standards. Contest winners were often recognized in the company-wide employee newsletter and sometimes receive a small monetary award as a token of appreciation.

Pitfalls to Creating Service Standards

By now, it is abundantly clear that I believe it is a waste of time creating and communicating service standards that are not applicable to all employees at every level. Your service standards cannot be perceived as an initiative *just* for the line and support staff. If senior leaders are not committed to also aligning their behaviors with the service standards, your entire service excellence initiative will be a failure.
Here are other common pitfalls:

- *Our standards are only for the employees who deal with external customers*
- *Our standards do not apply to managers*
- *Our standards are only applicable when you are in the presence of a customer*
- *Our standards do not apply to employee-to-employee interactions*

Key Points

- A major shortcoming of organizations is that they *assume* that once the organizational vision, mission and business objectives are in place, employees will automatically know those specific behaviors that are expected of them.

- Brand standards and service standards are not the same thing.

- Total employee involvement is the best way to ensure buy-in and support of your organizational service standards. The worst thing any organization or leadership can do is create service standards in a silo.

- Every level of the organization must be committed to demonstrating and energizing the service standards. They are not created just for line employees or support staff.

—◈—

CREATING THE BASIS
FOR SUSTAINABILITY
Part 2

The Six Principles of Service Excellence™

Vision/Mission Business Goals Service Standards	Part I CREATING THE BASIS FOR THE CULTURE
Intervention Selection **Learning Strategy** **Organizational Alignment**	**Part II** **CREATING THE BASIS FOR SUSTAINABILITY**
Measurement Leadership Accountability	Part III CREATING THE BASIS FOR CREDIBILITY
Role of the Leader Personal Application	Part IV TOOLS TO DRIVE SERVICE EXCELLENCE

A Feeling of Euphoria

After completing Part One of *The Six Principles of Service Excellence,* the refinement or creation of vision and mission statements, business goals, and service standards, *there is always a feeling of triumphant, absolute euphoria.* Part One involves a lot of purposeful work, and after completing the foundational principles for achieving service excellence, it is easy to assume nirvana has been reached.

Certainly, when you complete the tasks in Part One, you will have accomplished a great deal. But, remember the spinning plates? After all your hard work, this is no time to allow what you have set in motion to lose momentum and crash. Unfortunately, that will likely happen – unless you proceed immediately to Part Two and create a basis for sustainability. Beginning the intervention selection, learning strategy, and organizational alignment processes without delay is the only means of maximizing and preserving the exceptional accomplishments of Part One.

— ◈ —

INTERVENTION and
LEARNING STRATEGY
Chapter 6

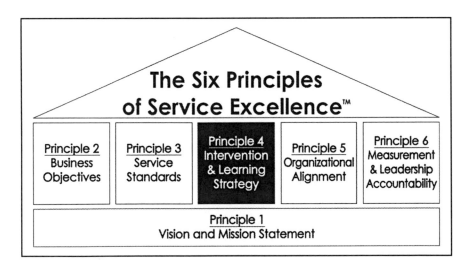

You must have a sound strategy and possess the right resources (people, work processes, tools, machines, technology, and work environment) in order to systematically drive service excellence and create sustainable change.

What is an Intervention?

In the context of service excellence, I define an intervention as a *solution.* This solution could be any identified process, resource, or tool that could be critical to closing the gap between mediocre and superior employee performance. Examples of service excellence interventions typically used to close employee performance gaps include:

- Implementing a structured customer problem resolution program
- Designing a comprehensive leadership development program
- Redesigning the new employee orientation program
- Creating a repeat customer recognition system
- Training employees on a new work process
- Re-evaluating your current employee recruitment and selection/ interview process

The most important tip to keep in mind is no intervention or solution should be implemented without at least first conducting a mini-gap analysis to determine the root causes of mediocre performance. Conducting a gap analysis will truly reveal those barriers impeding your organization and workforce from achieving service excellence. The closer you study a gap, the clearer you see how a single barrier can create a ripple effect that diminishes effectiveness of multiple segments within your organization. In this chapter, I have also included a list of questions that typically surface during a mini-gap analysis.

> - *Findings from the Service Excellence Study conducted by Performance Solutions by Design revealed that only 11 percent of the organizations polled currently integrate their service philosophy (vision and mission) with their foundational human resource practices (recruitment and hiring new employees, technical and soft skills training, performance management, reward and recognition, leadership development).*

> • *Only in five percent of those organizations polled are service excellence initiatives considered part of their annual company-wide strategic plan.*

Four Common Barriers

There are four common barriers to achieving performance and service excellence: (1) selection; (2) skill and knowledge; (3) work environment; and (4) reward and recognition. Typically a thorough gap analysis will uncover at least two or three of them.

Selection – Too often leaders do not link poor selection of new hires to mediocre customer service. There is, however, a direct connection. If service excellence is the goal of the organization, leaders must work diligently to select and hire employees who fit the profile. Doing this often requires waiting or "holding out" for the right individual.

> *Gap Analysis Question: Does your current selection process aid or hinder your ability to select employees who naturally embrace your organization's service philosophy?*

Skill/Knowledge – Most leaders place 95 percent of their training focus on technical skills. While technical proficiency is of great importance, in order to achieve service excellence, you must also continuously equip your workforce with the skill and knowledge necessary to consistently enhance the service experience for your customer. These skills include using: effective problem/conflict resolution; proper verbiage, and telephone etiquette; and service philosophy training, as well as other skills customers expect employees in your line of business to possess.

> *Gap Analysis Question: What percentage of your current training places emphasis on the service philosophy (vision, mission, service standards) of your organization?*

Work Environment – Frequently leaders are not held accountable for fostering a work environment where service excellence can thrive. The primary role of leaders is to ensure that their teams have the proper resources (right number of people to do the work, proper tools or equipment and effective work processes) to provide a quality product or service. When employees do not have the basics necessary to get the job done, resentment of both the leader and the organization develops. Just as proper selection and training are necessary to achieve service excellence, the work environment also plays a critical role in the equation.

> *Gap Analysis Questions – What is the "temperature" of your work environment? How satisfied are your employees with*

the current work environment? Does it support your service excellence initiative?*

Reward and Recognition – Employees who consistently provide exceptional service deserve reward and recognition – but do not always receive their due. While I will avoid getting into the issue of whether reward and recognition should be monetary or not, I definitely state it should be in a form that is viewed as highly desirable, something worthy of effort. Without reward and recognition, employees have no motivation to consistently demonstrate the behaviors that enhance the customer experience. A good service excellence initiative also includes how people who consistently go above and beyond will be rewarded and recognized. Keep in mind the key word is *consistency*! When consistency is lacking, your people will read the lack of it as favoritism; therefore, their motivation to excel will wither.

> *Gap Analysis Question: What method does your organization have for recognizing exceptional service? Is it effective? Is it consistent?*

Gap Analysis / Root Cause Identification

When analyzing the gap, a good starting point is asking your leaders, and perhaps your exemplary employees, to rate their ability to effectively service your customers on a regular basis. Honestly, even world-class organizations, such as The Ritz-Carlton, often rate themselves mid-range because they know that there is always room for improvement.

The Six Principles of
Service Excellence™

How would you rate the current level of service provided to your customers (internal or external) **on a regular basis?**

- **Superior Service (5)**
- **Mediocre Service (3)**
- **Substandard Service (1)**

The next step is to enlist feedback from the same group and ask each member to list or identify some of the barriers that diminish the workforce's desire and ability to consistently provide an exceptional service or product. To be candid, this process risks stepping on an occasional toe. Nonetheless, without honest feedback, it will be nearly impossible to determine the most effective and efficient interventions to develop and implement.

You will quickly find that some of the barriers surfaced by your employees and leaders are due to: *lack of a clear vision, and mission, inconsistent selection of new employees, no leadership accountability, inconsistency in service delivery, poor communication of work goals, lack of commitment from employees, or no employee empowerment.*

Interventions that Work

The Six Principles of Service Excellence is not a concept concocted in my head, one that has never actually been applied. In my consulting firm, these six principles are the foundation for all work we do with our clients, as well as how we operate internally. To show you that the concept works, I have outlined below real examples of interventions that have been successful for my clients within their first year of working with my firm. All of the clients cited involved a cross-section of their exemplary employees and leaders in identifying their organizational gaps, as well as the interventions necessary to close them.

INTERVENTIONS SELECTED	Golf Operation	Law Firm	Luxury Condo	Medical Facility	Bank	Auto Dealership
New Service Philosophy – created a new vision, mission, and service standards for the organization.			X	X		X
Revised Service Philosophy – revised the organization's current vision, mission, and service standards.	X	X			X	
Service Excellence Workshop - retrained all employees and leaders regarding new service philosophy *(vision, mission, business objectives, and service standard*s) in a half-day workshop.	X	X		X	X	X
Service Excellence Manager – selected a leader who is responsible for coordinating all efforts to drive and sustain the service excellence initiative within the organization.		X		X		

		X				
Leadership Development - implemented a comprehensive leadership development program to increase the effectiveness of their managers.		X				
Departmental Accountability Process - conducted follow-up meetings and held departments accountable for implementing a service excellence action plan.		X		X		
Customer Satisfaction Survey - conducted an initial survey to obtain baseline customer satisfaction data. Will continue to survey customers quarterly to determine improvements.	X				X	
Employee Service Excellence Survey – conducted a mini-survey to get employee feedback concerning service.				X		X

Employee Recognition Program – enhanced recognition program to support consistent demonstration of service excellence.	X	X		X	X	X
New Employee Orientation – revised orientation to align the program with the new service philosophy.	X	X	X	X	X	

The Process of Creating a Learning Strategy

The purpose of a learning strategy (which also can be referred to as an action plan) is to help you outline how to effectively implement your established interventions. Without a learning strategy, the identified interventions seldom come to realization. An effective learning strategy puts accountability to the test because it charts the course to your desired destination by the easiest and most logical route.

If you are lucky, your organization already has an effective strategic planning format or process in place, one that can easily be modified to fit the needs of a learning strategy. Whether or not this is the case, outlined below are a few items that should definitely be included when you develop your learning strategy.

Intervention – Detail what solutions will be developed and implemented to close current service gaps. Remember that these are the things we have identified, which will help you move from mediocre performance to consistent superior performance. *Interventions can include, but are not limited to: developing a service excellence workshop for all employees; improving your employee selection process; enhancing your leadership development program; implementing a new customer problem resolution process; conducting an employee and/or customer satisfaction survey,* *new equipment, or facilities; and implementing a new quality improvement initiative.*

Project Owner – Establish who will be in charge of ensuring the identified interventions are properly implemented. If you do not specifically assign someone this responsibility, the likelihood of a successful implementation is significantly diminished. *The project owner should be someone who is committed to and familiar with the chosen type of intervention.* For example, if the plan is to enhance or develop a new employee orientation, the most likely candidate for the role of project owner is your training manager.

Project Timeline – Establish when the intervention is expected to be completed and implemented. Project timelines should be reasonable and are necessary to ensure the project moves expediently. Without a project timeline, there is no way to hold the owner accountable for not getting the job done. *If a new process is being developed, I suggest a 90-120 day timeline. When enhancing a process that is currently in place, typically 30-60 days is sufficient.*

Action Steps – The steps that must be taken to implement this intervention should be spelled out. Even steps that seem apparent should be written to ensure everyone is aligned with what needs to be accomplished. This is an element of the learning strategy that should not be taken lightly but should be fully discussed with the project owner and the development/implementation team. *Steps that are often left out of the learning strategy are the pilot and evaluation processes; both are critical to sustaining the intervention's success.*

Champions – Establish which individuals are instrumental to the successful implementation of this intervention. This varies, based on the intervention; however, listing names helps the team identify those individuals whose buy-in and influence will be of benefit to them. *Your champions are not necessarily those involved in the development and implementation; however, their endorsement brings great credibility to what you are trying to accomplishment.*

Benefits of the Intervention – Articulate the reason the intervention is being implemented. During the service excellence journey, someone will ask why. Being prepared is your best defense. Preparing to answer the question prior to becoming involved forces the project owner and development team to determine if the intervention is worthwhile. Being prepared with an answer is also a great selling point when pitching a new intervention to senior leadership or to your identified project champions for approval and buy-in. *Examples of benefits could include: the intervention will increase employee loyalty; increase customer loyalty; reduce waste and operating costs; deliver quality improvement; increase revenue and profit.* The benefits, also, often coincide with the business objectives.

Process for Keeping the Intervention Energized – Consider and spell out ways to keep the intervention energized over the next twelve months. Remember, a service excellence initiative should not be perceived as a "program of the month." Therefore, a strategy must be in place to keep it energized in the hearts and minds of the workforce until it becomes second nature to them. *Ways to keep the intervention energized include: employee recognition; bulletin board or newsletter communication; employee general session topic; measurement and recordkeeping.* Many of these ideas will also become part of your organizational alignment process.

Example: Learning Strategy

Intervention	Project Owner	Project Timeline	Action Steps	Champions
New Employee Orientation: Integrate our new service philosophy *(vision, mission, service standard*s) into our current New Employee Orientation presentation.	Theo Jamison (Director of Training)	February 1st – March 1st	▪ Revise New Employee Orientation information. ▪ Update PowerPoint Slides. ▪ Pilot the new presentation with a cross-section of existing employees. ▪ Refine based on feedback. ▪ Implement March 2005.	▪ Company Executives ▪ Departmental Leaders ▪ Existing Employees

What Happens When There Is No Learning Strategy?

As I have emphasized throughout this chapter, the purpose of creating a learning strategy is to ensure a sound action plan is in place to support and sustain your service philosophy. There is no quick fix in this process; so, it does take time. When organizations rush to accomplish, they often totally eliminate this process, which sabotages the entire service excellence initiative.

Common pitfalls of not having a learning strategy in place:

- *Rushing to accomplishment without proper planning*
- *Wasted time and money on ineffective interventions*
- *No accountability for execution of the intervention*
- *Ineffective implementation of the intervention*

Learning strategies are most effective when they are closely linked to business objectives, vision, mission, and service standards. Still, again and again, I see organizations make the mistake of rushing to create or apply a customer service training program before knowing what the business goals are or uncovering the root causes of mediocre to poor performance.

Strategies that don't work can have the negative affect of diminishing your people's incentive to improve. An exceptional learning strategy will not only outline what training will occur over the next six-to-twelve months, it will indicate barriers to implementation and ways to overcome them. It will also include a list of internal champions necessary to execute the plan, and specify what other resources *(especially financial)* will be necessary to assure desired results.

Assessment of Your Learning Strategy

If you have some form of learning or implementation strategy in place and do not want or plan to reinvent the wheel, here are some questions that might help you assess its effectiveness.

- *What is your plan for providing employees with the skills and knowledge necessary to execute the vision, mission, service standards, and business objectives?*
- *Who is involved in designing the learning strategy?*

- *How do you hold leaders accountable for execution of the strategy?*
- *What type of buy-in and support is there from the top?*
- *How can the current learning strategy be enhanced?*

The learning strategy process is also a great opportunity to delegate tasks to leaders or team members to ensure the strategy is properly executed. It could even become part of the leader or team members' performance evaluation.

Key Points

- The purpose of a comprehensive learning strategy is to properly apply remedies, solutions, or interventions to close the gap between current performance and what is expected, based on the organization's business objectives, vision, mission, and service standards.

- Developing an effective learning strategy is key to creating sustainable change. In developing the learning strategy, you must look at the current state of training, work processes, and the work environment to determine where the performance gaps lie.

- A comprehensive learning strategy will also help identify workforce skill and knowledge deficiencies that impede achievement of business goals. The positive affect on employee morale, pride, and joy is amazing, when you provide them with the proper resources to get the job done.

- Creating the learning strategy must be a collaborative effort involving the departmental leader, departmental trainer and the training manager (if this role exists in your organization).

- What is the difference between a learning strategy and a strategic plan? Not much, except a learning strategy focuses on the action steps necessary to provide employees with exactly what they need in the way of skill and knowledge development. Without the steps and development, they will be unable to raise the bar and do an exceptional job of providing unparalleled levels of service.

- As in the steps of creating a culture of service excellence (vision, mission, service standards, business objectives, and intervention selection), involving employees in the planning of work that affects them is crucial. Who knows better than the line-level staff what they need in the way of knowledge and skill development to meet or even exceed the expectations of their leader, their internal customers, and their external customers? This is where key decision makers should also be intimately involved, as many initiatives involved in developing a sound learning strategy require adequate budgeting and financial backing.

ORGANIZATIONAL ALIGNMENT
Chapter 7

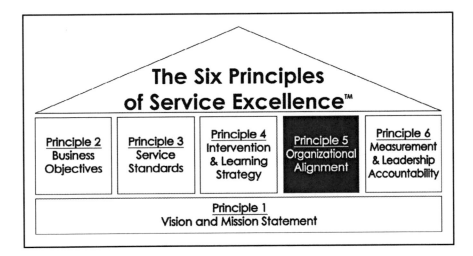

The Six Principles
of Service Excellence™

| Principle 2 Business Objectives | Principle 3 Service Standards | Principle 4 Intervention & Learning Strategy | Principle 5 Organizational Alignment | Principle 6 Measurement & Leadership Accountability |

Principle 1
Vision and Mission Statement

Without one hundred percent leadership focus, commitment, and accountability, service excellence with not thrive.

Repeat, Repeat, Repeat

Allow me to repeat myself: when implementing an effective, robust service excellence initiative, you can never communicate with employees enough. Years of research conclude that the more specific information is repeated, the more likely people are to retain and commit it to memory. If service excellence is important to your organization, do not allow anyone to make the false assumption that your employees will grow weary of hearing about it. People only tire of hearing the same message when it comes across as phony or disingenuous because no one is held accountable for living it. Talking sincerely about service excellence daily makes everyone at every company level responsible for energizing it.

As a leader, one of your major roles is to ensure that employees stay aligned with the philosophical values of the organization so that everyone marches to the same tune. The question becomes to what tune are you actually marching?

In organizations where employees consistently hear the CEO and other senior executives talk at length about revenue, profit and stock value, that is where the employees' attention and focus lie. Of course, these subjects are extremely important; others are, as well. The CEO and senior leaders must spend equal time talking about the value of customer loyalty and how exceptional service benefits every stakeholder from the employee, to the customer, to the community-at-large. When service excellence becomes a primary focus of senior leadership, it astoundingly becomes a primary focus of the entire workforce at every level.

Key Priorities are Seldom Misunderstood

I recently talked with a colleague who works for a large, financially successful global manufacturing organization; however, the company struggles with service and product quality issues. Again and again, they have tried to improve these two areas but have had little success.

When I asked what the CEO talks about the most, my friend answered, "The stock price. Every memo that comes from his office deals with market share, stock prices, profitability." She added, "When he does visit our business units, he never asks about our customer or employee satisfaction scores or what we're doing to improve quality; so, our employees don't really consider service one of his key priorities. But, the company's financial status? He always makes it a point of discussing it, good or bad."

Excellence in service and quality becomes a priority only when a CEO talks about service and quality until he is blue in the face; this is the essence of organizational alignment. It is about aligning the workforce with service, quality, revenue, and profitability because they not only affect the bottom-line, they also create a new dimension of customer loyalty.

In every industry, there are far too many examples of CEOs and senior leaders placing all of their effort on increasing profits, market share, and pleasing the shareholders, while leaving customer service issues in the often unreliable hands of employees who have received little or no direction or guidance. Just take a look at the next CEO interviewed on television and listen to where his or her focus is. If it is solely on finances, I guarantee there is little or no focus on customer loyalty at the mid-manager and front-line staff levels. I believe that any CEO and senior leadership deeply desiring customer loyalty can never overstate the importance of creating and sustaining a work environment that fosters service excellence.

What is Organizational Alignment?

Organizational alignment is taking full advantage of every possible resource to continually educate, reinforce, and remind employees of those key factors that are vital to a company's success. Daily line-ups or weekly pre-shift meetings, monthly departmental meetings, employee newsletters, company bulletin boards, intranet communications, and every training opportunity should deliver the message that creating loyal customers through service excellence directly contributes to financial success.

A good organizational alignment initiative makes certain that leadership is on board and continually relays the message to the foot soldiers, your front-line employees, keeping them focused on the purpose of their job – not just its functionality. In contrast, when there is no organizational alignment, you create a work environment that is negatively bursting at the seams, due to employee disempowerment, mistrust, and disengagement.

On a recent business trip, my colleague and I arrived at our hotel extremely tired, having experienced luggage and rental car problems at the airport. We looked forward to grabbing some dinner and a good night's rest. As we entered the hotel's lobby, the two front desk employees were preoccupied with the computer system, and it was several minutes before they decided to stop what they were doing and serve us.

"Name please," one of the front desk employees barked, as she proceeded to check us in. When we received our room keys, we realized we had been assigned exterior rooms on the first floor. Being female travelers, safety is always a priority for us; so, we asked to be moved to interior rooms on the second floor. The employees' non-verbal response was not overtly rude; still there was some huffing, puffing, and rolling of eyes as the employees gave us new room assignments.

As we rode the elevator to the second floor, I opened the hotel room key folio to discover the chain's "customer promise" signed by the CEO and Chairman. What I read made me feel cheated. It said, "We promise to always make you feel welcomed, provide the highest quality standards, respond promptly to your needs, and make you want to return."

You may be wondering what this incident has to do with organizational alignment. The simplest, most obvious, response is that it has everything to do with organizational alignment. I am certain that a dedicated team at their corporate offices spent considerable time creating this customer promise. Furthermore, the promise probably fits well with the company's vision and mission. The problem is that no one has taken the time to ensure that this customer promise stays engrained in the hearts and minds of every employee through regular communication.

Most likely the front desk employees we encountered had not seen or heard about the company's customer promise since they attended new employee orientation, which could have been years earlier. Sadly, this story is a real life example of what can occur when there is no process for ensuring every employee within a system is consistently aligned with the service culture and philosophical values of an organization. Consequently, customer loyalty simply isn't created.

The Simplest, Yet Least Used Step

No employee comes to work with the intention of being disengaged with co-workers or customers. However, leaders often do not give employees a reason to be engaged. Organizational alignment benefits your business by appealing to the hearts and minds of employees through open communication and dialogue. The process creates opportunities to regularly connect employees with their purpose in a meaningful and non-intimidating way.

The fifth principle in *The Six Principles of Service Excellence* is organizational alignment. While this is likely the simplest principle to implement, it is also the least used because leaders operate under the false assumption that, after you tell employees about the philosophical values one time, they will stick with them evermore. Organizational alignment is more than setting up a proper communication system to unify the workforce; it is also keeping everyone energized and dedicated to service excellence forever!

Since much time is invested in the development of new initiatives and strategies but very little time goes into the thought process of how to remain aligned, let's consider the opportunities you likely already have for easily integrating your service excellence initiative into your contact with employees:

- *Internet / Intranet Communication*
- *Internal Newsletters*
- *Daily Line-Ups*
- *Weekly Management Staff Meetings*
- *Monthly Department Meetings*
- *Quarterly "All Employee" General Sessions*
- *Visual Tools (Posters, Wallet Cards, Desk Tent Cards, Pins)*
- *Employee Handbooks*
- *Standard Operating Procedures*

When there is no solid communication or organizational alignment strategy in place, service excellence initiatives tend to fall off the radar screen within two-to-three months. To ensure your initiative is not perceived as temporary, you should use a variety of communication channels to keep the initiative energized for the long-term.

Because people learn, retain, and react to information differently, no one form of communication will always work best; therefore, what does work best is using all of them. Several studies show that people retain 90 percent of what they hear and see when the learning is multifaceted and interactive.

Assessing Organizational Alignment

A service excellence study conducted by Performance Solutions by Design, found that only five percent of the organizations polled have a consistent, effective process for continually aligning employees with the function and purpose of their jobs – which is daily delivery of unparalleled service. This means that 95 percent of the organizations polled were not regularly discussing and communicating the importance of their philosophical values.

If your organization does not have processes in place to align employees with service excellence, later in this chapter I will share some recommendations for getting started. However, if your organization already has processes for this purpose, the following questions can help you access their effectiveness:

- *What means of communication do you currently use to align the organization with the vision, mission, business objectives, and service standards?*

- *On a scale of 1-to-5, with 5 high, how effective are the tools employed at achieving your goal?*

- *Are you getting the results you expect?*

- *Who is responsible for executing the communication strategy?*

- *Are they capable of aligning the organization with the service philosophy?*

- *Can the communication strategy be enhanced? How?*

Creating Organizational Alignment

Just like any other process within *The Six Principles of Service Excellence*, creating organizational alignment takes a comprehensive approach. To create synergy and foster positive buy-in throughout the organization, I offer the following four suggestions:

Involve a Team of Employees in the Process - Even if someone is currently responsible for internal communication, I am sure he or she would welcome the assistance of a team. As with other teams we have discussed forming, this one should be small and for the sole purpose of fostering the organizational alignment for the service excellence initiative. The team should consist of five or six exemplary employees and leaders, all of whom should be volunteers. If you let it be known through your communication channels that you are actively seeking volunteers, you may be surprised at the volume of response you receive and the quantity of talent from which you can select. The reason for selecting from volunteers, rather than appointing the members of the team, is you stand a far better chance of assembling a dedicated group that will give the mission its very best. Still, even volunteers need to be kept energized; so, openly recognize and reward them once the process is in full swing.

Determine What Currently Works and What Doesn't - Have the team assess the company's current communication tools to determine the best venues for consistently energizing the service excellence initiative and the service philosophy. Questions the team might ask include:

- *What do we currently use that works?*
- *Are there companies that do a better job of internal communication than we? If so, what do they do?*
- *What will we communicate?*
- *How often will there be communication?*
- *When and with whom will we run a pilot to test the new process?*
- *How can we obtain and use employee feedback?*
- *How can we enlist the support, participation, and buy-in of senior leadership?*
- *How can we keep the information fresh, fun, and exciting?*

Pilot, Get Employee Feedback and Measure Effectiveness - Before implementing the organizational alignment process, I highly recommend conducting a pilot with a small, willing department or business unit. This allows for employee feedback and refinement of the process before implementing it company-wide. Also, piloting eliminates negative reaction by letting employees know up front that the process will be tweaked until it meets everyone's needs before being implemented. Typically, you will only get feedback from 20 percent of the workforce; however, the point is to give everyone a reasonable opportunity to have a say about the new process. Lastly, the team should plan to survey employees at least once a year to find out what they think, how they believe the process can be improved, and which service excellence topics they want added.

Make This a Long Term Strategy - Keep in mind, your organizational alignment process is intended to be in place forever. So, at some future time, you will need to consider whether it might be more effective to assign this responsibility to a single individual. If this is the direction you want to take, I recommend you still start with the team concept to allow time for the selection of the right individual with the right talent for this significant responsibility. The team's organizational alignment process should become part of the service excellence action plan or learning strategy talked about in Chapter 5. This ensures that team members are held accountable for getting the job done and that the process doesn't dissipate after two or three months.

Organizational Alignment Benchmarks

Organizations that are the most successful at implementing and sustaining service excellence through organizational alignment have a few things in common, they:

- *Assign* an employee who is responsible for overseeing the organizational alignment program. When there is not a specific individual accountable for the program, it does not last more than a few months.

- *Select* the best methods for organizational alignment of the service excellence initiative and use them consistently. Examples include: daily line-ups, weekly line-ups, employee newsletters, posters, wallet cards, etc.

- *Create* an editorial calendar with a minimum of six months worth of information. This will ensure proper planning of weekly topics and allow time to solicit information from departments, managers, and employees.

- *Determine* how often the information will be distributed, to whom, who will review the information at the department level, and what will happen to non-compliant departments.

•*Benchmark* and recognize the best practices of those departments that take the organizational alignment process to the next level.

The Ritz-Carlton Hotel Company is an excellent benchmark example of organizational alignment because its leaders consistently do a phenomenal job of aligning all employees through a daily line-up. At the beginning of every shift, all employees within a department gather for a brief ten-to-fifteen minute meeting. These meetings are called line-ups because everyone stands the entire time, which ensures the meeting does not extend beyond fifteen minutes. In most departments, the daily line-up is facilitated by the departmental leader. However, some departments rotate the line-up facilitator role, giving everyone leadership experience and adding variety. The daily line-up topic is selected by the Corporate Manager of Internal Communications, written and distributed to the hotels once a week via email. The Ritz-Carlton instituted daily line-ups as motivational and informational tools more than 15 years ago; so, they are pros at the process. After all these years, daily line-ups continue the process of keeping the philosophical values of the organization energized in their 30,000 employees.

Performance Solutions by Design schedules its organizational alignment meetings for every Friday morning at 9:30am. The meeting takes about 15-20 minutes, because it is held once a week, as opposed to daily. The weekly topic and discussion information is prepared every Wednesday by our Operations Manager who enjoys the tasks and is very skilled at it. She then forwards our weekly organizational alignment information to all employees via email so they can review and be familiar with it in advance. Our Operations Manager also facilitates the meeting, which covers our Service Standard and Core Covenant of the Week, discussion of how we can actively bring these standards and covenants to life daily, and any other business information that everyone needs to know. All staff members are expected to attend our organizational alignment meeting, no exceptions. Those employees who travel out of town are expected to call in by telephone to listen and participate in the meeting, if their schedule permits. We make time to recognize any employee who has recently gone above and beyond to take care of a client need, and we always end each meeting with a quote of the day that is linked to the topic of the week and our philosophical values.

Age Defying Dermatology, a highly regarded organization in San Jose, California, has also enjoyed success in implementing daily lineups. Although the organization implemented the line-up concept less than two years ago, the feedback from their employees is extremely favorable and proves effective in aligning everyone with the service philosophy. Age Defying Dermatology does not have the benefit of hiring an individual responsible for internal communication; so, the responsibility is rotated among their seven managers, weekly.

All the organizations mentioned above have also integrated service excellence into their selection process, new employee orientation, technical training programs, departmental meetings, all employee general sessions, and much more. Their diversified method ensures that no employee is left out because it is inclusive of everyone and ingrained within the work environment and company culture.

Benefits of Organizational Alignment

I hope I have done a decent job of articulating key benefits of implementing an organizational alignment strategy for sustaining a culture of service excellence within your organization. For those of you who need further convincing, it will make certain that:

- Employees understand their purpose versus their function
- Leaders live the philosophical values
- Everyone from the CEO to the janitor values the service excellence concept
- Everyone understands his or her role in achieving customer loyalty
- Everyone is held accountable for service excellence
- No room is left for excuses when customer service is deficient or lacking

Key Points

- In implementing an effective, robust service excellence initiative, you can never communicate with employees enough, especially if you expect employees to consistently deliver an exceptional service experience to each customer.

- Years of research indicate that the more you repeat specific information, the more likely individuals are to retain it. If service excellence is important to your organization, you must have an effective communication process in place to consistently keep the organization's philosophical and service values in front of your workforce.

- Organizational alignment is about setting up a proper communication system or process to align employees and keep them energized around service excellence forever!

- When there is no sound communication or organizational alignment strategy in place, service excellence initiatives tend to fall off the radar screen within two-to-three months. To ensure your initiative is not perceived as a "program of the month," you must have a number of communication systems or processes in place to keep the initiative energized and alive for the long-term.

—◈—

CREATING THE BASIS FOR CREDIBILITY
Part 3

The Six Principles of Service Excellence™

Vision/Mission Business Goals Service Standards	}	Part I CREATING THE BASIS FOR THE CULTURE
Intervention Selection Learning Strategy Organizational Alignment	}	Part II CREATING THE BASIS FOR SUSTAINABILITY
Measurement **Leadership Accountability**	}	**Part III** **CREATING THE BASIS FOR CREDIBILITY**
Role of the Leader Personal Application	}	Part IV TOOLS TO DRIVE SERVICE EXCELLENCE

Part Three of *The Six Principles of Service Excellence* focuses on measurement and leadership accountability, emphasizing the need for creating an effective measurement system capable of holding leaders accountable for service excellence. Measurement is

the only certain means of determining the return on investment of the service excellence initiative.

As you will see, working on measurement and leadership accountability demands a certain level of maturity in the service excellence journey. Once Principles One through Five are in place and well established, the final steps are to measure success, communicate it to senior leadership, and recognize and reward employees and leaders alike for contributing to the success of the organization's service excellence initiative.

—◈—

MEASUREMENT AND LEADERSHIP ACCOUNTABILITY
Chapter 8

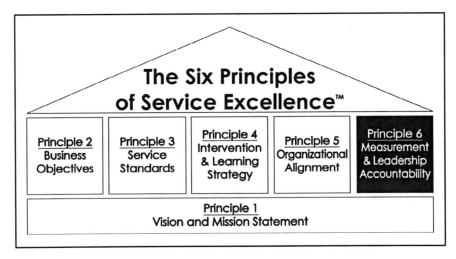

The Six Principles of Service Excellence™

Principle 2 Business Objectives	Principle 3 Service Standards	Principle 4 Intervention & Learning Strategy	Principle 5 Organizational Alignment	Principle 6 Measurement & Leadership Accountability

Principle 1
Vision and Mission Statement

Using Measurement to Build Credibility and Accountability

During the implementation of a service excellence initiative, measurement and leadership accountability are often overlooked. Therefore, the sole purpose of Principle Six is to determine the return on investment from the initiative and to help you maintain leadership's support and buy-in. It transforms your service excellence initiative from being perceived as a training program to being understood as an initiative of substance.

During the measurement process, we quantify the tangible results of your service excellence initiative in terms of improved employee productivity, quality, customer loyalty, sales and profit, in order to determine its success. Without an effective measurement tool or process for holding leadership accountable, the entire service excellence initiative reduces to no more than *a good thing to do.*

Create Simplicity, Not Complexity

Setting up a measurement process or scorecard makes it easy for leaders and employees to focus on the purpose of service excellence and determine its contribution to the organization's success. In terms of service and quality, it lets everyone in your organization know exactly what his or her job performance will be measured against; no one has to guess.

Service excellence measurement scorecards vary from one organization to the next, depending on the service and performance indicators chosen. However, they should be simple, easy to read, and easy to update. If you create a scorecard that is too sophisticated or complex, no one will use it for very long.

The service excellence scorecard format preferred by most of the organizations that I work with allows them to simultaneously track both improvements and shortcomings, using customer-related and employee-related data. In all categories, these scorecards start with current or initial data, then set annual targets or goals. Throughout the year, they track progress to determine if and where adjustments to the plan need to be made. Organizations that are more mature in their service excellence journey tend to track data quarterly, as opposed to semi-annually. However, there is no solid rule on follow-up intervals; it simply depends on what works best for your organization.

Service Excellence Scorecard				
SERVICE/ PERFORMANCE INDICATORS	Initial (January)	Mid-Point (June)	Annual (December)	Annual Goal
▪ Customer Satisfaction	72%	75%	82%	80%
▪ Customer Loyalty	8%	10%	15%	20%
▪ % Customer Defects	30%	15%	8%	10%
▪ Problem Resolution (Customer Satisfaction)	60%	65%	75%	70%
▪ Employee Satisfaction	60%	70%	75%	80%
▪ Employee Turnover	35%	28%	25%	20%
▪ # Internal Promotions	0	5	8	10
▪ Leadership Turnover	20%	15%	10%	10%
▪ Service Excellence Survey	60%	75%	85%	80%
▪ # Employee Good Ideas Implemented	0/month	10/month	12/month	5/month
▪ Sales/Revenue Increase	8%	10%	16%	15%
▪ Profit Increase	5%	8%	12%	10%

I am not advocating that this is the only format to use for your scorecard. However, here is a simple test for any scorecard. Ask yourself: *Could I easily explain our scorecard to a seventh grade student in three minutes?* If the answer is no, then your scorecard may be too complex. This applies, whether you work for a hotel, manufacturing company, financial institution, non-profit organization, or an engineering firm. Simplicity is always more sustainable than complexity.

If your organization already uses a scorecard or other measurement tool to track customer service, employee productivity, revenue, and profit and your scorecard is very effective, I recommend you make it the model for your service excellence scorecard. Most leaders and employees like recognizable things in the workplace, and merely modifying what is already in use will ease everyone's frustration level.

Where Do We Start?

If scorecards are a new concept to your organization, simply start by identifying data that is currently being measured. A well developed service excellence scorecard should help you gather all of this data into one central, easy to review document. Does your organization currently track customer satisfaction, employee satisfaction, sales, and profit, as well as types of customer problems and their frequency? If the answer is yes, start with a scorecard that tracks these service indicators. If the answer is no, initiate a cross-functional team of leaders and employees to surface easy ways to start tracking the information, then pilot the plan during the first year. In the second year, refine your scorecard; by then, you should have reliable baseline data or information.

As your organization matures and service excellence becomes a part of your culture, add more sophisticated measurements, such as customer loyalty, employee engagement, percentage of customers satisfied with how employees resolved their problems, product quality indicators, and so forth. However, I cannot overstate the need to keep the scorecard simple during its first year of implementation.

Recognizing Top Performers and Helping Low Performers

In creating your service excellence scorecard, realistic year-end goals must also be set with input from employees. Valuing their observations and frontline experiences keeps them involved and contributing to the process.

Another major factor is having a recognition process for rewarding departments or teams that consistently exceed the established goals. Keep in mind that reward and recognition programs do not have to be a huge financial burden on the organization. They can range from monetary incentives, such as gift certificates, to a pizza party for the department. Be sure to add a feature article and team photo in an issue of the employee newsletter so that everyone is aware of the accomplishment. You will be surprised at how far a little recognition can go toward rallying an entire organization to excel in service. Your service excellence initiative should be perceived by leaders and employees as a positive, fun, and engaging way to help reinforce good customer service practices – not as another cumbersome project to be implemented.

There must also be an *improvement strategy* in place to help departments or teams that fall below the established goals. This will show that your organization is uncompromising and serious about service excellence. The goal of an improvement strategy is not to punish low performers but to outline and implement realistic action steps to get them in line with the rest of the work force. I cannot imagine a work environment where a department or team deliberately wants to be perceived as bringing the service excellence scores down for the entire business unit. When people understand how they rank in comparison with their colleagues, low performers work diligently to do whatever it takes to catch up quickly.

Anytime I encounter an organization that is having trouble sustaining service excellence or quantifying their return on investment, I find the problem always links back to not having processes or systems in place to keep track of and handle low performing departments or individuals. Subsequently, when top performing departments see that the non-performers are not held accountable the service excellence initiative steadily fades throughout the organization.

I am sure you are right now asking yourself, "So, what do you do to bring low achieving teams and individuals into line?"

I once encountered such a dilemma. As a Human Resources Director of a mid-sized hotel I found myself consistently counseling a particular manager about the low-performance of his team. We finally reached a point where his rationale and excuses for low performance were no longer acceptable and were significantly lowering the customer loyalty scores of the entire division. After much thought, I decided to work with him to devise an improvement plan.

We first looked at his department's service excellence scores in relation to the other departments within his division. Then we synergistically created four simple action steps to get his team on track and a timeline for implementation of the action steps. I made it very clear that if improvement was achieved within a reasonable amount of time, the team would be publicly recognized and commended. I further clarified that if no improvement was made, our next meeting would be a heart-to-heart discussion concerning his inability to drive service excellence within his team and a subsequent job reassignment to a non-leadership position would be impending.

After a 90-day period, the manager and his department were finally on track with the rest of the organization because he took the improvement plan approach seriously. He went back to his team, shared the action plan, and made minor tweaks based on their feedback. Once everyone realized that the support of the entire organization was behind them and everyone wanted to see them succeed, a renewed sense of pride and joy filled the department. As a matter of fact, one year later, this department went on to be the benchmark of service excellence within the hotel. By working together to identify and close their service gaps, they became the premier department that everyone admired, and, today, that leader is a General Manager of a reputable hotel chain.

Holding Leaders Accountable
for Service Excellence

That story also applies to leadership accountability, which is the final element in implementing a successful service excellence initiative. Most management incentive programs involve measurements such as: *employee and customer satisfaction, labor turnover, profit and loss, customer problem resolution, internal defect and waste reduction, industry and community recognition awards.* All of these measurements should also be incorporated into your Service Excellence Scorecard. When elements like these become part of leaders' incentive, they immediately begin to understand their role and importance in sustaining service excellence. They also understand the purpose of their work far better; thus, they become dedicated, key contributors to the success of their teams and of the organization as a whole.

With a few minor adjustments, your organization may already have some of the service excellence scorecard elements in place. Success is virtually assured when you acknowledge leadership accountability and performance with a reward and recognition program that is based on the success of the service excellence initiative and meeting or exceeding the scorecard goals.

Leadership Expectations

I believe that every employee has the capability to be a leader. I say this because in the context of *The Six Principles of Service Excellence,* leadership is not a position; it is a mindset and a pattern of behaviors that influence and inspire others to achieve greatness.

I worked with a healthcare organization that implemented a service excellence initiative over a twelve month period. They rewrote the organizational vision, mission, business objectives, and service standards. Then, they trained everyone on the new service philosophy. Also, they implemented daily line-ups to ensure employees stayed focused, energized, and aligned. While employee engagement and customer loyalty were growing remarkably, the CEO was still not satisfied with the progress being made. She felt something was still missing.

As we began to peel back the onion, we surfaced two major root causes of her dissatisfaction. First, we found that although her leaders were one hundred percent committed to the service excellence initiative in their hearts, they were inconsistent in their actions. Often, during peak business demands, they would turn a blind eye. Through tacit approval, they allowed employees to compromise the newly established service standards. Second, we found that the leaders were not living up to the expectations of the CEO. As hard as they tried, they could never meet the CEO's expectations, largely because those expectations were never articulated; no one knew exactly what they were.

To resolve these issues, we worked with the CEO and her leaders to develop leadership expectations so that it was clear to the leaders what was expected from them. Now, the CEO can confidently hold everyone accountable for consistently driving service excellence. She uses their semi-annual management performance reviews, quarterly bonuses, and other leadership incentives as a means to hold them accountable. There is no assumption of what the leaders think the CEO is looking for; they now know specifically what leadership actions and behaviors are important and they are aware of the rewards of meeting or exceeding these leadership expectations, as well as the consequences of being considered a low performer.

If you are facing a similar situation, I recommend you consider drafting leadership expectations for your organization and getting leadership feedback before adopting and implementing them.

Leadership Expectations for Performance Solutions by Design

In support of our service excellence initiative, every leader within our organization is expected to consistently:
- *Demonstrate commitment to our service philosophy and operating principles*
- *Lead change initiatives that positively support our business strategy and positively communicate reasons for change*
- *Hold themselves and others accountable for achieving excellence*
- *Address conflict in a timely manner*
- *Set and reinforce team goals that support our business strategy*
- *Proactively identify and remove barriers to achieving greater organizational and team performance*
- *Hire for talent and skill to build a high performing team that supports service excellence*
- *Foster open communication and empowerment to create a self-reliant team that has a customer first focus*

Creating the Basis for Credibility

It is only reasonable for any organization's CEO and senior leaders to be interested in quantifying the return on their investment in a service excellence initiative. Following The Six Principles step-by-step provides concrete proof of the process's ability to succeed, build customer loyalty, and pay great financial dividends. In fact, I know of no organization that has followed them all and not realized success on multiple levels. It seems so elementary – yet it is so easy to overlook the connection between achieving service excellence and increasing customer loyalty and employee loyalty. Loyalty on both sides of the equation creates profit, and profit is the goal of any sensibly run organization. Consistent dedication to an accurate measurement process and leadership accountability keeps all parties mindful of the role that service excellence plays in a great organization.

Assessing Measurement and Leadership Accountability

To help you assess the affect of your organization's measurement tools and ability to hold leadership accountable for service excellence, ask the following questions:

- *Do you conduct stakeholder (customer, employee, supplier, and owner) satisfaction surveys?*

- *What are your goals for improving your survey results?*

- *What is your process for holding employees accountable for reaching these business goals?*

- *Is your organization's employee accountability process effective? Does it get the results you expect?*

- *Do your surveys measure key factors related to the organization's mission, vision, business objectives, and service standards?*

- *How can your current scorecard be enhanced?*

- *Do your leaders know exactly what the CEO expects from them?*

If the majority of your answers were unfavorable, I suggest you revamp your measurement process so that you can appropriately hold your leaders accountable.

The Power of Visual Reinforcement

After the new or enhanced service excellence scorecard is finalized and adopted company-wide, I strongly recommend you employ your organizational alignment process as a means of communicating the new measurement tool and ensuring everyone is aware of their heightened level of responsibility and accountability. Enlarged service excellence scorecards should be posted throughout the offices and other work areas to keep employees updated on the progress or lack there of.

If your organization consists of a number of departments or business units, we suggest you post both the company-wide scores and departmental scores. This creates a great spirit of competition and positive peer pressure. Remember, no one ever wants to be identified as the low performer.

Key Points

- During the implementation of a service excellence initiative, measurement and leadership accountability are often overlooked.

- The sole purpose of Principle Six is to determine the return on investment from the initiative; which is typically of greatest interest to senior leadership and helps maintain their buy-in and support, while building credibility.

- A service excellence initiative without an effective process to measure its effectiveness fails to hold leaders accountable and results in a poorly executed, short-lived project.

- Setting up a measurement process or scorecard makes it easy for leaders and employees to focus on the results of service excellence. In terms of service and quality, it helps them know exactly what their job performance will be measured against.

- Any organization having trouble sustaining service excellence or quantifying return on investment invariably lacks a process or system capable of tracking and handling low performing departments.

— ◈ —

NECESSARY TOOLS TO DRIVE SERVICE EXCELLENCE
Part 4

The Six Principles of Service Excellence™

Vision/Mission Business Goals Service Standards	**Part I** CREATING THE BASIS FOR THE CULTURE
Intervention Selection Learning Strategy Organizational Alignment	**Part II** CREATING THE BASIS FOR SUSTAINABILITY
Measurement Leadership Accountability	**Part III** CREATING THE BASIS FOR CREDIBILITY
Role of the Leader **Personal Application**	**Part IV** **TOOLS TO DRIVE SERVICE EXCELLENCE**

Part Four of this book is dedicated to helping you overcome any personal barriers or gaps that may be standing in the way of your ability to achieve excellence. Together we will explore leadership's responsibility and role in driving service excellence, as well as, taking a personal approach to applying *The Six Principles of Service Excellence.*

These are the building blocks for beginning to execute or implement everything you have learned throughout the past eight chapters of this book. The necessary mindset to drive service excellence is one of openness and willingness to break your previous paradigms and discover new ways to create a more meaningful life, both personally and professionally.

THE ROLE OF THE LEADER IN ACHIEVING SERVICE EXCELLENCE
Chapter 9

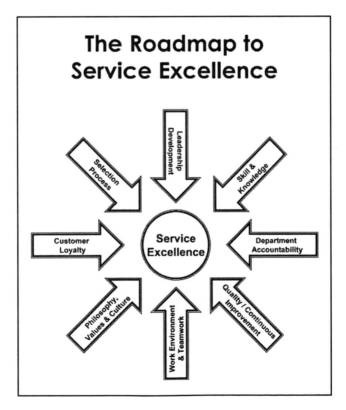

The Roadmap to
Service Excellence

Leadership Development

Selection Process

Skill & Knowledge

Customer Loyalty

Service Excellence

Department Accountability

Philosophy, Values & Culture

Work Environment & Teamwork

Quality / Continuous Improvement

> *Predominantly, what keeps leaders from achieving service excellence is their inability to change their paradigms.*

Leadership's Responsibility

When it comes to service excellence, I am extremely hard on leadership because they are all too often the *root cause* of mediocre or poor service experienced by the customer. I know this is a hard notion to embrace; however, it requires changing your paradigm about leadership accountability to truly surface the source of bad service provided by your organization. You can do just that by asking *why* five times. Here is a real example involving a restaurant chain that brought me in for consultation. I asked three of their exemplary employees the following questions:

- **Why is service so terrible at this restaurant?** *Because most of the employees have a bad attitude.*

- **Why do employees have a bad attitude?** *Because they don't like serving customers.*

- **Why don't they like serving customers?** *Because service is not a natural attribute of theirs.*

- **If service is not a natural attribute, why are they in front-line service positions?** *Because the restaurant was short staffed and the manager quickly hired the first group of applicants available.*

- **Why would the manager do that?** *Our assumption is because management does not value the customer enough to ensure the right employees are in front-line service positions. Therefore, the manager is not willing to wait for the right candidates to fill the jobs. Also, our manager does not hold current employees accountable for delivering good service.*

While, in the context of the entire book, this chapter may seem redundant, leadership's responsibility in achieving and sustaining excellence can never be overstated. The role of the leader in achieving service excellence is to champion the cause. If leadership – everyone from the CEO down to the supervisor – is not committed everyday to being the walking, talking embodiment of service excellence, the initiative will not be taken seriously within the organization. Instead, it will be perceived as a passing fad.

Whenever I provide consultation services for organizations that are diligently working to implement service excellence initiatives, I always insist we start service excellence education at the top with senior leadership and work our way down through the rank and file to the front-line employees. I never assume that leadership clearly understands or regularly demonstrates all of the characteristics that are necessary to achieve service excellence. If they did, a strong service philosophy would already be meticulously woven into the fabric of the workplace and organizational culture. There would be no need for a special initiative to address service gaps or barriers because there would be no gaps.

Benchmarking Excellence in Leadership

If you are consumed with providing the ultimate service experience for your customers, most likely you have already studied world-class service organizations, such as Disney and The Ritz-Carlton. I can tell you first hand that these revered organizations firmly believe in and make it a priority to hold their leaders accountable for exceptional internal and external service. Their leaders are held to the highest level of accountability for:

- *Hiring employees who enjoy serving others, and find delight in anticipating and exceeding the expectations of the customer*

- *Ensuring customer loyalty is the ultimate goal of their team*

- *Living, eating, and breathing the organization's service culture, philosophy and values*

- *Creating a work environment where employee empowerment and teamwork thrive*

- *Seeking opportunities to continuously improve the quality of products and services*

- *Being committed to continuous learning through leadership development opportunities*
- *Ensuring their team has the necessary skill, knowledge, and resources to take service to an unparalleled experience for the customer*

Organizations with a strong service culture seek out the best leadership talent – not only from a technical perspective but also based on ability to complement the organization's service philosophy. Leaders are not allowed to give excessive excuses when their business unit fails to meet operational, quality, financial, or service excellence objectives. Everyone knows up front what is expected of them, and they also know the consequences of continually failing to meet expectations.

Leadership Self-Assessment

The greatest value of this chapter is helping you assess your individual ability to affect service excellence within your organization, division, department, or small work team. In other words, before you can effectively help others improve their leadership skills, you must first *honestly* identify and address your own strengths and weaknesses, as they relate to service excellence.

Take a few minutes to complete the following mini-assessment. It will help you evaluate both your ability and that of your leaders. Only check those statements that you strongly agree with, meaning you are 100 percent confident it is a true statement about your organization.

THE SIX PRINCIPLES LEADERSHIP ASSESSMENT		
I / My	Our Leaders	Principle #1 – Vision and Mission
		Know the vision and mission of the company
		Talk about the vision and mission in staff meetings
		Recognize employees who reinforce the vision and mission in their work
		Act as a role model of the vision and mission

		Immediately challenge employees who do not energize the vision and mission at work
		Work Contributes to the vision and mission
		Employees understand that the work they do contributes to the vision and mission
		Employees support the vision and mission
I / My	**Our Leaders**	**Principle #2 - Business Objectives**
		Know the business objectives of the company
		Talk about the business objectives in staff meetings
		Reinforce the business objectives of the company
		Work contributes to achieving the business objectives
		Employees understand that the work they do contributes to the business objectives
		Department goals are aligned with the business objectives
I / My	**Our Leaders**	**Principle #3 - Service Standards**
		Know the service standards of the company
		Regularly talk about the service standards in staff meetings
		Recognize employees who reinforce the service standards in their work
		Have the resources to consistently deliver the service standards
		Act as a role model of the service standards
		Employees regularly demonstrate the service standards
		Immediately challenge employees who do not demonstrate the service standards
		Hold employees (at every level) accountable to the same service standards

If you checked all of the statements under each principle, your organization is a benchmark that exemplifies service excellence.

In such a case, I only recommend periodic reinforcement through employee and team recognition to sustain the culture.

If you checked at least six of the statements under each principle, your organization is well on its way to achieving service excellence. Therefore, I recommend periodic internal auditing to ensure consistency, as well as stepping up the recognition of employees who consistently demonstrate the organization's service philosophy.

If you missed five or more statements under each principle, there are a number of barriers preventing you from achieving service excellence. I recommend you reevaluate the effectiveness and consistency of all that has been done to date and make immediate changes.

Leadership Qualities that Support Service Excellence

In Chapter Two, a considerable amount of time is spent outlining the characteristics leaders must possess in order to support, drive, and achieve a culture of service excellence. However, these nine characteristics bear being briefly repeated because the leaders you select to execute your initiatives have great bearing on your success. If your organization does not start with leaders who naturally possess these qualities, you are starting with a crippled workforce and at a disadvantage.

- *Leaders must be avid students of service excellence*

- *Leaders must find meaning and purpose in their work*

- *Leaders must find intrinsic satisfaction in watching employees grow and thrive in a work environment that fosters empowerment and uncompromising levels of service*

- *Leaders must stay focused on the big picture, the long-term objectives*

- *Leaders must set high standards and hold employees accountable for attaining them*

- *Leaders must be competitive and desire to consistently be number one*

- *Leaders must know that their attitude (good or bad) sets the tone for the team*
- *Leaders must be empathetic in their helpful approach with people*
- *Leaders must have a natural desire to share knowledge with their team*

An Uncommon and Continuous Pursuit

The CEO and Director of Sales of a prominent hotel and conference center organization in England spent significant time benchmarking some of the renowned organizations in the United States and went back to their leadership team with a number of best practices that they wanted to implement. After about of a year of developing and communicating their new service philosophy's vision, mission, and service standards, as well as implementing new processes for new employee selection, new employee orientation, performance management, and daily line-ups, they called on me for further guidance.

Quite frankly, after reviewing all of the new information and processes they had successfully integrated into their culture, I was very impressed and at a lost as to why they needed me. However, after working with their leadership team to assess their service gaps and barriers, we came to the conclusion that their leaders were only able to create pockets of excellence because they were not holding employees accountable. Nonetheless, I was extremely impressed with the progress they had made prior to my working with them.

Over the next three months, we implemented a few, simple, accountability interventions and tightened up some of their internal processes to ensure service consistency. They are now working at a higher level. Their drive, sense of urgency, and execution strategy were unmatched by most of the American companies for which I had consulted. In fact, I have not seen such passion and commitment to achieving excellence since working with The Ritz-Carlton organization.

Keep in mind that this is a small organization with seven hotel and conference centers spread throughout England. Their workforce consists of roughly 500 employees, and very young managers. In spite of their young leadership team, some of the strengths that make this organization an exceptional benchmark of service excellence include:

- *Strong, unwavering support of the service excellence initiative from the CEO. He set the team charter, moved out of the way, and empowered his Service Excellence Team to build on his vision.*

- *A highly competent Service Excellence Team, consisting of a general manager and two training managers. All are equally passionate and driven to improve service and employee performance.*

- *Excellent vision and mission statements, and service standards are already in place.*

- *A strong sense of urgency and eagerness to immediately improve and implement processes that would close service gaps.*

- *A solid Employee Induction Program (new employee orientation) that makes every new employee an instant believer in the service culture and philosophical values.*

- *A structured daily line-up process, designed to ensure that every employee (new and existing) is aligned with the company's service culture and philosophical values.*

Because of these simple strengths, I predict that within two years this organization will become a global benchmark for service excellence, just as The Ritz-Carlton is today. The benefits they gain include increased employee loyalty, employee empowerment, and retention, as well as increased customer loyalty, revenue, and profitability. All is being accomplished because they consistently endeavor to create a work environment that will foster and sustain a higher level of service for all concerned.

Most leaders go into a service excellence initiative thinking it will take decades to attain the prominence and success of organizations such as The Ritz-Carlton or Disney. The conference center example illustrates that, with the right leadership and a strong sense of urgency, great things can be accomplished in a short period of time. Their accomplishment is a great testament to the fact that oftentimes *simplicity fosters excellence, while complexity fosters mediocrity.*

Reasons Why Service Excellence Initiatives Fail

Implementing a service excellence initiative is like baking a cake. Suppose you were commissioned to make the most wonderful wedding cake money could buy. However, you were limited to only a few of the necessary ingredients and utensils: flour, eggs, water, and a mixer – but no sugar, baking powder, butter milk, or mixing bowl.

Just as you must have all of the proper ingredients and equipment to create a delicious cake, with a service excellence initiative, you, likewise, cannot cut corners. Nonetheless, many organizations that aspire to be like The Ritz-Carlton, fail to invest all the essential ingredients, not realizing the solid, unwavering commitment necessary for success.

As a consultant, I am often asked to create an unparallel customer experience in some given industry. That I can do; however, like the baker given limited ingredients, I cannot succeed without the essentials: people, processes, tools, and technology.

The odds of successfully implementing a service excellence initiative are stacked against most leaders and organizations due to the following reasons:

- *90 percent of senior leaders aspire for their organizations to be better*
- *80 percent of senior leaders will send someone to benchmark a world-class organization*
- *70 percent of leaders will share the information from their benchmarking experience when they return to work*
- *60 percent of leaders will get approval to implement a full-fledged service excellence initiative based on the feedback they bring from the benchmarking experience*

- *50 percent of leaders will lose interest in the initiative or get distracted by other pressing issues before setting up the first team meeting*

- *40 percent of leaders will become overwhelmed, decide that this type initiative is over their heads, and not move forward after the first meeting*

- *30 percent of leaders will begin to cut corners in implementing the initiative, thinking: "We don't have to do all of that"*

- *20 percent of leaders will get promoted, transfer to another area, or leave the company altogether before the completion of the initiative*

- *10 percent of leaders will fully implement the initiative and be successful*

As the odds show, the success rate of an endeavor of this magnitude is extremely low because organizations or leaders start cutting corners almost at the onset of the initiative. There are many reasons for the failure rate, many of which are exact opposites of the strengths of the hotel and conference center I worked with in England. Here are just a few I have encountered.

Lack of a sense of urgency: Waiting too long to implement an initiative or an intervention slows momentum, and the whole idea eventually grinds to a halt. A lack of urgency is the reason that at least 50 percent of all service excellence initiatives are unsuccessful.

Disempowerment: Senior leadership's unwillingness to empower its hand-picked Service Excellence Team to make decisions allows internal bureaucracy to stagnate the initiative. Ninety percent of the time the problem is the team's lack of empowerment to make decisions on behalf of senior leaders. Often this is due to senior leadership's failure to select the most competent, trusted team members from the onset.

Fear of Change: When leaders fear that changing and communicating a new service philosophy will produce a negative effect, they tend to cling to the old, irrelevant vision, mission, and service standards – assuming they ever existed. This includes the fear of losing non-conformant employees who are unwilling to accept change – even if it is for the good of the organization.

Lack of Accountability: When there is no consequence for not conforming to the new service philosophy, there is no consistency in service, and ultimately the customer suffers. This creates an environment where employees perceive the service excellence initiative as a temporary program and do not bother to listen or comply.

No Discipline or Focus: When no one takes time to sit down and focus on ironing out the processes necessary to support excellence, the end result is just lip service from leaders, instead of action. The customer is, therefore, subjected to mediocre or poor service because senior leadership does not hold leaders accountable for immediately implementing the vital action steps necessary to improve service within their departments.

Lack of Tenacity: If leadership becomes consumed by the sometimes overwhelming task of implementing a service excellence initiative, inability to continue driving the initiative over the peaks and through the valleys overcomes the positive benefits of completing the project.

Leadership Action Plan

Once you have had an opportunity to assess your own leadership effectiveness, as it relates to *The Six Principles of Service Excellence*, the next logical step is to identify ways to close your personal leadership gaps. Questions you might ask yourself during this self-discovery are:

- *What potential barriers do I face in energizing service excellence within my division, department, or business unit?*

- *What resources might I need from senior leadership to overcome the barriers and accomplish my goals?*

- *What will I personally START, STOP, and CONTINUE in order to overcome these barriers and to enhance the service delivered?*

Service Excellence – Leadership Action Plan			
I can START	**I can STOP**	**I can CONTINUE**	**RESOURCES I can use**
•Citing examples of how the work our department does contributes to the company's **vision** and **mission**.	•Assuming employees understand the vision and mission.	•Talking about the vision and mission of the company in my departmental meetings.	•A poster of the vision and mission hung in our department.
•Regularly reviewing the **business objectives** with my staff.	•Assuming employees are able to link the company's business objectives to the work they do everyday.	•Monitoring and evaluating employee performance based on the business objectives.	•A clear explanation of the new business objectives from senior leadership.
•Challenging employees who do not consistently apply or follow the **service standards**.	•Accepting substandard work by allowing negativity and mediocrity to fester within the department.	•Leading by example. Reminding employees of our service standards.	•A copy of the service standards added to the technical training manual so it is reinforced as part of skills training.

Developing your individual leadership action plan will also provide you an opportunity to bring together everything you have learned about service excellence and, then, set a course of action. I urge you to make a pledge to yourself to implement your action plan immediately – not a week or month later – today. Also, tell someone about your plan, preferably a colleague you trust, someone who will hold you accountable for doing what you have said you will do.

Understanding Leadership's Purpose

For leaders who are able to clearly distinguish the difference between their purpose and function, *The Six Principles of Service Excellence* concept will come easy; their concepts of leadership revolve around empowerment and change, which are natural, everyday parts of life for them. On the other hand, leaders, who focus solely on refining the technical or functional aspects of their jobs, often get promoted and become good technicians; however, they are rarely able to truly inspire their employees to achieve greater goals. If they are successful at doing so, it is often through intimidation, coercion or threats.

The Six Principles of Service Excellence™

Leadership Function	Leadership Purpose
Manage and oversee department or division operations	Inspire, lead and motivate employees to achieve greater goals
Operate within budget	Set the vision and mission for the department, division or work team
Hire and manage employees	
Attend meetings	Be a mentor, coach and role model
Control costs and waste	Ensure the team is aligned around a common purpose
Maintain and improve worker productivity	Provide direction, praise and recognition for a job well done
Handle internal/external conflict	Develop the skill and talent of their team
Complete reports	
Maintain safe work environment	

Leaders, who focus on both the function and purpose of their jobs, work at a higher level of effectiveness and efficiency. They are astute, concerning the technical skill and knowledge necessary to drive the business, but they also possess a natural, keen sense for motivating their team to exceed the company's expectations.

Think about a time when you worked for a leader who was solely focused on the functional aspects of his or her job; how did it feel? That leader was probably a good person but not someone you would go above and beyond to please, impress or make proud of you. Now, think about a leader you have worked with who fully embraced both the functional and purposeful aspects of his or her work; how did that feel? Most likely the person who comes to mind is someone you now consider a role model. He or she was an excellent technician, practiced integrity, made you feel the work you did contributed to the greater good, and had a sense of urgency about work accomplishments. Therefore, you naturally desired to do more to please them.

I urge you to take a few minutes and jot down those aspects of your job that are functional, necessary to successfully get work done everyday. Then, jot down a list of things that define your purpose as a leader. After you have done so, look at the lists and determine where most of your time is spent. If it is on the functional aspects of your job, you will be limited in your endeavor to achieve service excellence and must look for immediate ways to balance both function and purpose.

My Service Excellence Role Model

During my hotel career, I once worked for a general manager who was clearly able to move from function to purpose at the drop of a hat. The functional aspects of his job were always apparent and well executed. He was a world-renowned hotelier, revered by leaders inside and outside of the hospitality industry, one who held all leaders under his direction accountable at the highest level for the manner in which they ran their department or business unit. He was often intolerant of excuses for budget deficits, low occupancy, staffing issues, lack of supplies, or any other barrier that we, leaders under his direction, thought prevented us from meeting our established departmental goals. He often said: "Excuses are for losers," and quickly dismiss any explanation (legitimate or not) that we had for not meeting his expectations. We quickly learned to be more proactive and become better business leaders through his actions. He was extremely consistent, never wavering in his vision, always linking customer loyalty and employee engagement to profit dominance in our industry.

You might think that working for such an individual would be unbearable; however, everyone who came in contact with him felt a high sense of admiration. Employees were so loyal to him they would move heaven and earth to ensure his success. His secret was this: In spite of all of the business demands of running a successful hotel, he still treated each individual with a high level of respect. It didn't matter if you were the pot washer or the director of sales, in his eyes everyone deserved the right to be treated with dignity. Each hotel employee understood that his or her job was valued and leaders understood that their jobs were to ensure their employees had everything they needed to be successful. While he was strict and unwavering about achieving business goals and objectives, he never neglected an opportunity to help leaders and employees understand the "why" or the motive behind their hard work. His diligence in helping employees understand the motive inspired them to do more and achieve more, which resulted in the start of an extremely successful hotel company and refined service culture.

Over time, this General Manager became President, then CEO, then co-Chairman of the organization and grew it from five hotels to 29. He never neglected an opportunity to immediately recognize employees who consistently exemplified the service philosophy of the organization. Also, he never missed an opportunity to correct or challenge leaders or employees who compromised service standards. He clearly enjoyed stepping into a training session or attending line-ups to clarify and align everyone with the vision, mission, and business objectives of the organization and make them simple enough to motivate even the housekeepers to do and achieve more.

When he recognized individual strengths and talents in leaders, he stretched them to accomplish more challenging tasks. He was a true mentor and coach to many because his job extended beyond the functional aspects of being CEO and moved into instilling a sense of purpose, not only in himself, but in every employee he encountered.

Key Points

- The root cause of poor or mediocre service is often ineffective leadership. If you were to *"ask why five times"* concerning poor service, the answers almost always links back to the lack of sound leadership.

- Organizations that are revered for consistently delivering unparalleled levels of service firmly believe in holding their leaders accountable for exceptional internal and external service to customers. Such organizations do not accept excessive excuses when a business unit fails to meet operational, quality, financial, or service excellence objectives.

- Before you can effectively help others improve their leadership skills, you must first honestly identify and address your own service strengths and weaknesses.

- Most organizations fail in their service excellence endeavors for three reasons: (1) they lack a sense of urgency to get the project completed; (2) they do not empower their Service Excellence Team to make decisions on behalf of senior leadership; and (3) they lack the tenacity to continue the endeavor, even in the wake of what may appear to be insurmountable challenges.

—◆—

APPLYING THE SIX PRINCIPLES
TO YOUR PERSONAL LIFE
Chapter 10

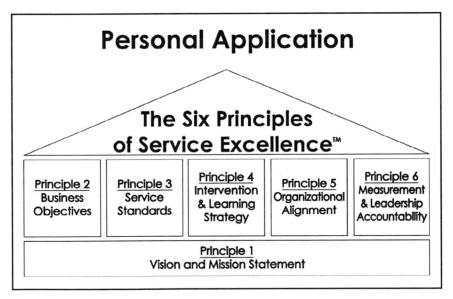

A Personal Approach through Self-Reflection

This chapter is not intended to teach you how to write a personal vision or mission. Based on what you have studied and learned thus far, you should have the foundational knowledge necessary to create those documents with some level of ease. The true purpose of this chapter is to address the need for applying the same principles that richly reward business to your personal life. We will take each of The Six Principles and guide you through how and why it is important for you to apply this body of knowledge to your personal life.

I am awed by how eloquently some leaders and employees are able to recite the vision and mission statements of their organizations. However, when asked, *"What is your personal vision?"* and *"What is your personal mission?"* many are at a loss for an answer. Most begin with a deep sigh of hesitation before honestly admitting they do not know.

Prior to writing this book, I never spelled out my personal vision statement; largely because I had never been challenged to do so. Ten years ago, however, after attending a workshop on *The Seven Habits of Highly Effective People*, I drafted my personal mission statement. That was the first time I had been confronted with truly defining my life's purpose beyond a list of things to do. And, believe it or not, the personal mission statement I wrote ten years ago is still relevant today.

I imagine a few readers still think it really isn't necessary to follow all of the principles in order to deliver excellent service. And, I am fairly certain that those same doubters don't see the point of applying The Six Principles to their personal lives. But, I submit to you that, if you are a leader who is consumed with achieving and sustaining service excellence in your organization, you are, likewise, consumed with the pursuit of excellence in your personal life.

Mahatma Gandhi is credited with saying, *"One man cannot do right in one department of life whilst he is occupied doing wrong in any other department. Life is one indivisible whole."* There is also a biblical quote that says, *"You cannot serve two masters. You will love one and hate the other."* I firmly believe that life cannot be effectively divided into two halves: one half professional and one half personal. Life in itself is whole; it is made up of the experiences and lessons learned by the whole person, not two half people.

Therefore, whatever you do or aspire to do professionally should correspond directly with your personal beliefs and values. When your personal belief system or values are compromised or contrary to what you are doing, it causes significant internal conflict for you both, professionally and personally. Applying *The Six Principles of Service Excellence* in your life requires deep introspective thinking and internalizing all that you have learned thus far.

To help you start this journey of self-reflection, here are a few questions I would like you to consider.

- **Principle 1 - Vision and Mission:** What is your vision for your life? What legacy do you aspire to leave? What is your personal mission? Is your personal vision and mission still in your head or carefully thought out and committed to paper?

- **Principle 2 – Objectives:** What are the four major goals you want to accomplish in your lifetime? Are they centered on your vision, and mission? Will they define success and life fulfillment for you?

- **Principle 3 – Standards:** What should you start doing today to ensure your behaviors and actions are synergistic with your personal vision, mission and goals?

- **Principle 4 - Intervention and Learning Strategy:** Where do the gaps exist between what you aspire to be and what you are today? If the gaps are many *(no time, lack of confidence, no sense of urgency, no vision – mission – goals, fear of writing them down, fear of not being able to live up to them, lack of funds),* what interventions do you need to implement in your personal life to close them? When will you start taking action? What resources will you need to stay on track? What is your action plan?

- **Principle 5 – Alignment:** Are your vision, mission, objectives, and standards written and posted in a place where you can regularly review them? Do you surround yourself with people who are like-minded and share the same or a similar vision, mission, and set of goals? Do you read, study, and apply knowledge that will help you stay on track?

- **Principle 6 – Measurement and Accountability:** How will you determine your success in living your vision and mission? How will you hold yourself accountable for your success?

These questions are not intended to make you feel a sense of failure or feel that applying these principles to your life is virtually impossible. These simple, yet insightful, questions are intended to cause a higher level of thinking and help you work toward personal accountability.

Personal Vision and Mission

Since age nineteen, I have aspired to be an entrepreneur. However, I knew it would take years of training and apprenticing under great mentors and role models to reach my vision. Only within the past twelve months have I been able to refine my personal vision statement and condense it to a concise sentence that reflects what I aspire for my life. My vision is *to create a global enterprise that will maximize my strengths and talents, while helping others to realize and achieve their dreams.*

My seventeen years with The Ritz-Carlton, as well as, other jobs and mentors along the way, have allowed me to experience a rich, stimulating life. It has also afforded me every opportunity to follow my vision, mission, and goals. At times in my career when I wavered from my destiny or core values and beliefs, I usually was not comfortable and didn't stay with those organizations very long. I am fortunate that those experiences were few. Over the last ten years, I have kept my mission statement accessible inside of my personal organizer/calendar, so I can review it periodically without wasting time searching for it.

My personal mission statement is a bit long. Even though it may not be the most eloquently written document I have ever created, I would not change one thing about it. Each time I read it, it continues to instill a sense of pride in me.

My Mission Statement

I will live each day with joy and excitement, looking toward the future. Never fearing past mistakes, I will learn from them. I will live within my imagination -- not from memory – and keep my life in harmony with nature.

My loved ones, dearest friends and other associates will view me as a responsible, highly effective, and caring individual who wants to help them realize their highest potential. I am willing to learn and understand their wants, needs and desires. Honesty, loyalty, love and integrity shall be the foundation for all relationships I enter.

In everything I do, I will always put my values first. In every decision I make, I will search for knowledge and wisdom. I will seek to understand the perspective of others and always search for a winning solution for all concerned.

Each day I aspire to be a key contributor in my church and community, and to help the underprivileged fulfill their dreams.

Personal Objectives

When applying The Six Principles in your personal life, be mindful not to confuse your personal objectives with a list of things to do. Just for a moment, I would like you to think about the things you want to bring about in your lifetime, the accomplishments that will not only add meaning to your world but could also enrich the lives and experiences of others.

Each year, like most of you, I make a list of personal goals. Typically, my list includes tasks such as paying off debt, exercising more, eating right, and completing continuing education classes that will increase my knowledge. However, as I dig deeper into personally applying The Six Principles, my lifelong objectives are to:

- *Acknowledge God's handiwork and divine intervention in everything I do*

- *Be a key contributor of time and money to my church and community-at-large*
- *Build a world-class enterprise that adds value to organizations and individuals*
- *Develop and nurture a supportive and compassionate relationship with my husband, parents, siblings, grandparents, and other extended family members*

Unlike the business objectives described in Chapter Four, my personal objectives are not quantifiable. What is most important is for them to be realistic, accomplishable, and synergistic with my personal vision and mission.

Personal Standards

At this point, it may be hard to distinguish the difference between personal objectives and standards because, as you begin to create them, they may sound the same. This is fine in the beginning; however, as you continue the process of self-reflection and searching inside to determine your destiny, the differences between your personal objectives and your standards will eventually be sorted out. As with service standards for organizations, our personal standards are those behaviors that, if followed, will guide us in the direction of achieving and living our vision and mission.

To effectively commit to paper your personal standards, you will need to review your vision, mission, and objectives. I suggest you have them all on a piece of paper in front of you, then start to think about all the things you need to do and be that are synergistic with your core values (vision, mission, objectives).

My Core Values	My Personal Standards
Personal Vision To create a global enterprise that will maximize my strengths and talents, while helping others realize and achieve their dreams.	I will run my business ethically, demonstrating the highest standards of professionalism so I am a role model for my employees and colleagues.
Personal Mission I will live out each day with joy and excitement, looking toward what the future holds. Never fearing past mistakes, but ever learning from them. I live within my imagination and not from memory. My life will constantly be in harmony with nature.	I will seek to understand and utilize the strengths and talents of my team, and apply that knowledge to raise their level of effectiveness.
My loved ones, dearest friends, and other associates will view me as a responsible, highly effective and caring individual who wants to help them realize their highest potential. I am willing to learn and understand their wants, needs, and desires. Honesty, loyalty, love, and integrity shall be the foundation for all relationships I enter.	I will support my colleagues, employees, and family in whatever positive manner possible to achieve their individual aspirations and goals.
In everything I do, I will always put my values first. In every decision I make, I will search for true knowledge and wisdom. I will seek first to understand the perspective of others and always search for a winning solution for all concerned.	I will not be afraid of failure nor allow the fear of taking calculated risks to prevent achieving excellence. I will acknowledge God's presence and divine intervention in everything I do and pursue.
Each day I aspire to be a key contributor in my church and community, helping the underprivileged fulfill their dreams.	I will be involved in activities that contribute to and promote the success of my church and community-at-large. I will be a life-long learner in order to enlarge my sphere of knowledge, skill, and determination.

Personal Objectives	
• Be a light and a key contributor within my church and community-at-large in time and money expended • Build a world-class enterprise that adds value to organizations and individuals • Develop and nurture a supportive and compassionate relationship with my husband, parents, siblings, grandparents, and other extended family members.	

Interventions and Strategy

Principle 4 – Intervention and Learning Strategy, deals with identifying any barriers that might prevent you from living your vision, and mission, achieving your objectives, or demonstrating them through your personal standards. Start by evaluating yourself; on a scale of one to five, with five high. How well are you doing at:

- *Living in alignment with your vision?*

- *Living in alignment with your mission?*

- *Reaching your personal objectives?*

- *Consistently demonstrating your personal standards?*

- *Driving these core values in your life?*

If you are not able to answer these questions favorably, I suggest you peel back the onion further to determine exactly what is preventing you from scoring yourself a four or five and what you are going to do about it. From experience, I can tell you that lack of personal time is often the biggest barrier. I freely admit that I sometimes have difficulty finding time to sit down and think introspectively about my life. The second biggest barrier is people not believing all of this is necessary.

I suggest that if you truly want to create balance in your life that you make time over a weekend or during your vacation to think about your life as a whole and work through some of these issues and barriers. Your greatest goal will be determining ways to overcome these barriers to ensure you are living a more meaningful and purpose-driven life.

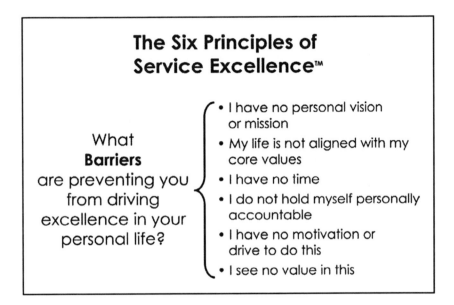

The Six Principles of Service Excellence™

What **Barriers** are preventing you from driving excellence in your personal life?

- I have no personal vision or mission
- My life is not aligned with my core values
- I have no time
- I do not hold myself personally accountable
- I have no motivation or drive to do this
- I see no value in this

I once worked with a colleague who was very successful professionally, and it showed in his six figure salary and quarterly bonuses. However, there was no sense of fulfillment in his personal life. He, frequently, stated that in order to maintain a successful career, personal relationships would have to suffer. At the end of the day, he often felt guilty because the imbalance between his personal and professional lives was the primary cause of deep conflict between him and his spouse. He felt like no one understood.

One day I asked him, "What is your vision and mission for your life?" In frustration he responded, "I don't know...I don't have time for that kind of stuff." After his frustration subsided, I suggested that not having "time" might be the root cause of imbalance in his life. After a few minutes of silent contemplation, he agreed with me and made a commitment: over the next two weeks he would make time to begin defining his core values, using The Six Principles concept and methodology.

Three weeks later, he came back to me proudly displaying his personal vision and mission statements, as well as his personal objectives and standards. He admitted that it was quite a task. However, making time to create these documents forced him to think deeply about his personal and professional life and how to find fulfillment, purpose and meaning in both. He, also, mentioned that he made certain his wife was included in the process, in order to make his vision and mission statements a family endeavor.

Now, when things don't seem to be going his way professionally or personally, he can always reflect on his mission and vision statements to ensure he is working in unison with them and not against them. He recently mentioned that his life is more complete and that he has a solid compass to base all of his decisions on. Now, his focus has shifted from just his professional life to a more holistic approach that includes his family, his church, and his community-at-large. He says that the greatest satisfaction he has gotten out of this endeavor is having a sense of purpose, meaning, and fulfillment.

Personal Alignment

To ensure that I stay on track with my core values, I often surround myself with family members, friends, and business associates who are likeminded. I have often found that when I am with people who think or act contrary to my core values it causes friction and conflict. I, also, read and study mostly books and articles that help motivate me to drive my purpose and meaning in life. The programs I watch on television are those that are analogous to my core values.

My intent is not to shelter myself from the realities of life; it is to avoid counterproductive relationships and experiences. Think for a moment about the people with whom you regularly associate, the types of information you read, what you watch on television, the clubs and associations you are part of, the places you frequent. Do they add balance or chaos to your life?

Measuring Success and Personal Accountability

In the final analysis, how will you determine your success or failure at achieving your vision and mission? I will measure my success to some extent based on what others feel, think, and say about me farther down the road.

When my grandmother turned eighty, our family threw a huge birthday celebration for her. Everyone was there. The room was filled with her children, grandchildren, great grandchildren, co-workers, childhood friends, church members, and neighbors. It was a joyous event.

During our tribute to her, just about everyone wanted a moment to say a few words about their relationship with her. Some of the words they used to describe her were: wonderful person, close-friend, role model, mentor, strong willed individual, feisty, compassionate, loving, cheerful, other-centered, generous, and giving. It was evident that she was highly admired by both young and old.

That day I was especially proud of my grandmother and thought to myself: that's the kind of legacy I want to leave. That day I realized that life is not necessarily measured in monetary value or by material gain, but in personal value and the role model you set for others to emulate.

If I want to be known as half the person my grandmother is, I must hold myself accountable for demonstrating the standards I have set for myself everyday. Yes, a portion of my success will be based on my ability to be a light, build a world-class organization, and develop supportive relationships with everyone I encounter. However, the largest measure of success will be based on what others have to say about me on my eightieth birthday or long after I am gone from this earth.

Conclusion

It is hoped that, by accompanying me on my personal journey with The Six Principles, you see that it is possible to apply this concept and its methodology to your personal life. It is not an easy task; however, it is achievable. I wish you much success in applying The Six Principles of Service Excellence in your organization and in your personal life.

— ◈ —

INDEX

CPSIA information can be obtained at www.ICGtesting.com
265369BV00002B/120/A